THE IDOL CALLED GRACE

BY DAVE VANCE

May God's grace
be ever sufficient
for you, in you, & for
you! Thank you for
shining grace so
beautifully! You
guys are a huge blessing!

Dave Vance

EQUIP PRESS

Colorado Springs

THE IDOL CALLED GRACE

BY DAVE VANCE

First Edition: Year 2019
The Idol Called Grace / Dave Vance
Paperback ISBN: 978-1-946453-53-2
eBook ISBN: 978-1-946453-54-9

What Others are Saying

OUR HEARTS AND MINDS PERPETUALLY produce idols of all sorts, but is it possible to make grace an idol? In this thought-provoking book, Dave Vance explores how we can make idols out of God's good gifts and challenges us not to put anything above God Himself. This book will help you evaluate what you worship and why.

Dr. Thomas White
President and Professor of Theology

DAVE VANCE ENTERS THE ANCIENT discussion on the often over-exercised subject of the grace of God with a much-needed fresh voice in his new book, *The Idol Called Grace*. Written from the heart of a pastor, yet from a mind of a seasoned theologian, Vance tackles the subject of grace from a perspective every committed believer needs to critically consider. From the first chapter, you enter the back door on the subject of grace and immediately find yourself called on the wrestling mat to grapple with the familiar doctrine. Each subsequent chapter then leads you further into the new arena of thought challenging your theological framework. By the end of the match, you emerge with a renewed perspective and love for the doctrine and the God who offers us His grace.

What I love about Vance's style is that it is engaging and readable for those new to walking with Christ while at the same time thought-provoking and deep, rich with doctrinal complexity to challenge even the seasoned believer. *The Idol Called Grace* is a breath of fresh air. It is for anyone who has grown weary of the shallow, easy-to-understand doctrine of grace that stains our contemporary churches and bookstores. This is a book that cannot be recommended highly enough.

Tim Armstrong
Senior Pastor of The Chapel in Akron, Ohio

DAVE AND I FREQUENTLY DISCUSS the need to challenge people to live a life for Jesus out of a personal faith rather than some other prime mover such as culture or personal benefit. In light of my regular discouragement with various books over the years, I am thrilled that Dave finally wrote this book. *The Idol Called Grace* may be one of the best resources I have found. From practical examples to deep biblical study, *The Idol Called Grace* will walk you through the dangers of worshiping grace as an idol and how surprisingly prevalent this trend is today. Furthermore, you may find traces of grace as an idol in your own life as I did. Whether you are surrounded by people who are living a cultural Christianity rather than a personal one, or charged to lead such a community of people, this book is a must read.

Rev. W. Bernt King Ed.D.

ACKNOWLEDGMENTS

I WANT TO THANK MY GODLY mother for introducing me to God's grace early and often in my journey. You have been God's hand of grace to me in your prayers, encouragement, and teaching. I still remember the night I heard you praying, "Lord, I don't know what to do with him. Take him…he's yours!" Thank you for the faith legacy you birthed in me.

Deep thanks to my "baby-love," my wife, Allyson, for the consistent picture of faithfulness that you reflect in your love, support, and shared dedication to Christ. In the darkest moments, you have been God's voice of strength and focus to keep going and a beautiful reminder that the cause is a worthy one. There is no one else that I would rather be on this grace-journey with.

Tremendous thanks to my four boys, David, Caleb, Jacob, and Isaac. Being your father has taught me more about grace than anything else in life. The grace-legacy that continues through you inspires me daily. My prayer is that God would constantly use you to go further and reach more than I could ever possibly imagine. May your lives reflect the great grace God has shown me through you.

I have had the privilege to serve in three amazing churches and lead two churches. Each church has been an amazing gift to my life. I especially want to thank the wonderful staff and people at Crossroads Church in Mansfield, Ohio, who have allowed me to grow and learn as their pastor. You not only have encouraged this project, but you have dreamed with me and displayed an amazing picture of what this book is about. It is one of the greatest honors of my life to be called your pastor.

There are so many that have graciously spent time reading and editing this project. Big thanks to my personal assistant, Nicole, and my co-worker and friend Doug for reading every word and sharing your honest opinions. I am also so appreciative of Michele, Stephanie, Kelsey and the team from Outreach Inc. and Equip Press for taking some random thoughts in my mind and making them a project worth sharing.

But by the grace of God I am what I am, and his grace toward me was not in vain. (1 Corinthians 15:10)

A GRACE-FILLED TENSION

T HERE ARE TIMES IN OUR lives where God calls us into tension. A tension found in our discovery of who he is and what he has done. In essence, it's an invitation into a wrestling match with the God of the universe. These moments when we enter the ring can be wonderful moments, but they also can be overwhelming. As a seminary student at Capital Bible Seminary, in Washington, DC, I had a systematic theology professor who provocatively challenged my thinking concerning how we view theological truths in the Scripture. He would say that whenever you study theology, you're left with what he called "blessed despair." "Blessed despair" describes the parallel feelings we have when studying the depths of God. On one hand, you feel so blessed, yet at the same time, it leaves you in despair. It leaves you wanting to bang your head against the wall. Why? Because we, the finite, are endeavoring to understand the infinite. And as we attempt to discover who God is, we continually run into our own limitations and inability to fully grasp the magnitude of his glory. So if we are to get in the ring with God, if you will, and wrestle a bit with who he is, I believe it has a way of stretching our minds, stirring our souls, expanding our thinking, and deepening our hearts.

Personally, there has probably been no subject that has caused me greater wonder, awe, and reverence, while at the same time more inquiry, contemplation, and searching, than the subject of grace. I mean, what is grace? What does it look like to live out grace? *Grace*...take a moment and ponder it. Isn't it such a common word in the Christian world? We use it all the time. Yet in spite of its repeated use, it would be safe to say that *grace* is one of the most beautiful and powerful words in our entire language, and at the same time one of the most mysterious foundations of our beliefs found at the core of Christian theology.

We see the beauty of grace fleshed out in our everyday lives. We hear it in our songs. It seems like not a day goes by without a worship song entering the scene with *grace* in its title. Old hymns like "Amazing grace, how sweet the sound, that saved a wretch like me" and "Grace, Grace, God's grace. Grace that is greater than all my sin" as well as newer songs, "From the creation to the cross. There from the cross into eternity. Your grace finds me" and "How wonderful, how glorious. My Saviors scars victorious. My chains are gone. My debt is paid. From death to life and grace to grace." Songs are written about it. Sermons also focus on it. Simply do a search on sermons about grace and you will find titles like... "More Grace," "Great Grace," "Amazing Grace," "Wonderful Grace," "Marvelous Grace," "Remarkable Grace," just to name a few. Churches have attempted to tie their purpose to the word *grace*. We find all kinds of churches with the word *grace* in their title. There are names like Grace Baptist Church, Grace Bible Church, Grace Apostolic Church, Grace Pentecostal Church, and Grace Church. I would bet that there is likely a church with the word *grace* in its title within forty miles of where you live.

It almost seems like *grace* is the word of the day. Why do so many talk about, sing about, and desire it? Because it's at the core of who we are. It's the centerpiece of our doctrinal foundation and our salvation experience. This one word expresses the experience of every Christian in every place, at every age, and in every language. And this is exactly what led me to some deeply rooted questions about our understanding of this concept of grace: how we see, describe, and discuss it. My hope is that these questions will be an invitation to join me in the ring with God as we wonder about and wrestle with our view of grace.

I have to confess, this conversation isn't the normal description of grace. Instead, we are going to look at grace from an entirely different perspective, a shadow side, if you will. I wonder, with all the uses of the term and concept of *grace* that we see in our culture today, is it possible that this magnificent concept can actually become dangerous? Is it possible that the very grace on which our lives rest has unintentionally risen to a place it was never meant to be? Could it be that we have so misaligned the grace of God that grace has actually become an idol? Has it become a spiritual golden calf that we attempt to worship above God himself?

Some of you see the words *grace*, *idol*, and *dangerous* used in the same sentence, and you might think that grace is like your mother-in-law showing up at your house without a Snickers bar.[1] You might even wonder, "Dave, have you lost your theological mind? Is this a vain attempt to get fired? Has ministry finally done you in, that you would describe grace as dangerous…as an idol?" No doubt, I deserve each of these questions. I confess that I didn't fully realize where this journey was going to take me. What I hope to do over these next few pages is to invite you into a wrestling match with grace and God. I'm not naïve enough to believe that you will agree with everything you will read within these chapters as we contend with this theological subject. What I am asking you to do is be willing to grapple with what God's grace looks like today in our world and in your life. Would you wrestle with what God's grace looks like doctrinally in Scripture and practically in your life? What I can promise you is that if you are willing to wrestle with the concept of grace in this way, I believe your understanding of grace will become fuller and your view of God will become even greater.

These types of questions aren't anything new. Throughout the centuries, key, core doctrines of our Christian heritage have been the subject of much debate. And probably no basic truth has caused more discussion and debate as the topic of God's grace. Questions like "What is grace?" and "What does a grace-filled life look like?" reveal our inquiry and also our confusion about the doctrine of grace. And what we know about doctrine, all doctrine, is that for every great point of articulation, there can also be a shadow side. There's always a dark side, a humanly twisted angle, and a manipulation of terms. I find this to be equally true about our understanding of biblical grace.

---

1   I love these series of commercials by Snickers. The commercial focuses on a person who isn't acting like their normal self. The commercial reveals them as another character who is cranky, frustrated, or angry. One of my favorites is where a young man is portrayed with a cranky Betty White. But when they are given a snickers bar, they transfer back to their normal selves followed by the tagline, "You're not you when you're hungry." These are certainly creative and hilarious commercials. Although, I have to confess that my statement is in no way a description of my own mother-in-law.

Our walk into the ring will bring us face to face with the dark, shadow, and unspoken side of God's great grace. Namely, how we tend to manipulate this magnificent word, abuse this beautiful concept, and twist grace for our benefit. Let me put this in foundational terms. I want to confront the notion and ask deep questions over the next few pages. **Have we relegated grace to merely a system of belief that has little impact on our behavior? Has grace become only an idea, a word, a song, a doctrinal point, or something that now stands on its own with little connection to the One who created it in the first place?** These are the questions…the invitation. I hope the answers will stretch you like they've stretched me.

TABLE OF CONTENTS

THE IDOL CALLED GRACE

BY DAVE VANCE

CHAPTER ONE

GRACE...AN IDOL?

N OW THAT YOU'RE READY TO throw this book away and label me a heretic, let me pause and begin to define some terms that will bring sense to what I am saying. Defining grace and idolatry could be a book in and of itself—thus we won't take the time to discuss the details about these subjects—but we need to at least be on the same page about what these terms mean. And I want to start with this term *idolatry*.

WHAT IS AN IDOL?

WHAT IS THE FIRST THING that comes to your mind when you think of the word *idol*?

When I hear the word *idolatry*, I immediately think of Indiana Jones chasing the Holy Grail in the well-known movie *Indiana Jones and the Last Crusade*. If you remember the end of the movie, upon reaching the mysterious temple, characters Donovan and Elsa use Indiana and Henry Jones, Indy's father, to maneuver past all the traps to reach the chamber of the coveted Holy Grail. Of course, Donavan and Elsa pick what they perceived as the most beautiful chalice studded in bright emeralds, causing Donavan to age to dust immediately. Upon his death, the guardian knight, who had been alive for seven hundred years by the power of the Grail, delivers this penetrating line, "You have chosen poorly!" What a great line! As expected, Indiana Jones selects the correct cup, an old wooden, humble, cup. But you know the thing that surprises me most about this scene? The Holy Grail mixed with the temple water constituted what they referred to as "living water," which holds eternal wisdom and eternal understanding. Hollywood couldn't be that obvious, could it? When we hear the word "idolatry," this is probably the picture that first comes to our minds. I know it is for me.

Or maybe, like me, you have visited a country with a history of idolatry. I think of a global ministry trip I took to Cambodia with a ministry partner called Asia's Hope.[1] On one such trip, I had the privilege of visiting a well-known temple site called Angkor Wat. Angkor Wat is the largest religious monument in the entire world. If you've ever watched the Discovery or History Channels for any extended period of time, you probably have seen Angkor Wat. It seems to appear on there weekly. It was built during the Khmer Empire and was originally dedicated to the Hindu god Vishnu. There are castles, pyramids, and tons of monuments inside. As you explore the many temples on the grounds of Angkor Wat, you cannot escape the numerous physical idols representing many different false gods. These stone relics represent different perspectives of these gods. There is one particularly interesting one that represents a replica of Vishnu, the Hindu god, with many different arms representing different aspects of deity. In another temple there was a combination idol of Vishnu and Buddha.[2] These are just a few of the many images of idolatry at Angkor Wat.

Likewise, stone relics, golden calves, and tiny statues are what most likely come to mind when I say the word "idol." And if that's true, then probably most of us would say, "I don't have an idol issue." I doubt anyone is reading this in front of a little trinket that you're burning incense for and chanting to, but that's precisely the image most of us have, and as a result, we think of idolatry as something distant from us. Something other-cultural.

But Scripture reveals something else. Something surprising. We find that idolatry is actually at the core of our identity. I love the description used by Martin Lloyd Jones, former pastor at Westminster Chapel in London. He gives us a helpful definition of idolatry: "An idol is anything in my life that occupies a place that should be occupied by

---

1   A great organization based out of Columbus, Ohio, that rescues orphans and connects them with a family.

2   In the twelfth century Buddhism took over, so all over Cambodia today you find a mixture of both Hindu and Buddhism together. Consequently, they combine the gods in a physical relic as half Buddha, half Vishnu.

God alone. An idol is something that holds such controlling position in my life that it moves and rouses and attracts me so easily, that I give my time, attention and money to it effortlessly."

Similarly, Pastor Tim Keller, founding pastor of Redeemer Presbyterian Church in New York City and best-selling author of *Counterfeit Gods*, said, "What is an idol? It is anything more important to you than God, anything that absorbs your heart and imagination more than God, anything you seek to give you what only God can give you... An idol is whatever you look at and say in your heart of hearts, 'If I have that, then I'll feel my life has meaning, then I'll know I have value. Then I'll feel significant and secure.'"[3] He goes on to say that anything can be considered a god if it rules and serves as a deity in the heart of a person or in the life of people.

Undoubtedly, there are many other nuances related to the definition of idolatry. But for the sake of our study, I want to combine these two definitions into a fuller, yet more specific definition, especially as it relates to grace.

> **Idolatry is exchanging what has been given by God to reflect his glory and satisfy our enjoyment in him for our selfish desires, our self-assurances, and our self-serving intentions.**

Please pay careful attention to each of the words used in this definition. Notice it takes the gifts God has given to us for his glory and for our satisfaction in him and uses them for our selfish assurances, our selfish desires, and our self-serving intentions. In essence, we exchange what God has given for self. It's as if we say, "I'll take that, God,

---

3   Tim Keller, *Counterfeit Gods: The Empty Promises of Money, Sex, and Power, and the Only Hope that Matters* (London: Penguin Books, 2009), xvii–xviii. I am indebted to Tim Keller for his source on the subject of idolatry. If you are looking to understand the concept of idolatry more deeply, this is the book for you.

and use it for me." That's idolatry at the core. Simply put, it is giving central value to something other than God in our lives.

Whether we like it or not, as a result of the sinful fall, we all have idol-making factories in our hearts. John Calvin, the great reformer, emphatically described this truth when he said, "The heart of a man is perpetually a factory of idols. Give us a chance, and we'll replace God with any and every object, any and every person, any and every idea, and any and every dream." And idolatry fleshes itself out in many different arenas of life, as we are going to see in a moment. But more importantly, the Scripture itself testifies to the difficult truth that we all have idolatrous hearts. In fact, some scholars believe this is such a prominent subject throughout the Scriptures that they would consider idolatry as the central theme of the entire Old Testament.[4]

You don't have to look far to find it. Consider the Law of God given to Israel. In Exodus chapter 20, God gives the Ten Commandments. Do you remember the first commandment? The first one is striking to say the least. Exodus 20:1–3 says, "And God spoke all these words, saying, 'I am the Lord your God, who brought you out of the land of Egypt, out of the house of slavery. You shall have no other gods before me.'" There it is. He says it in one verse, "You shall have no other gods before me." Why does God make this the first commandment of all commandments? Because God understood that the moment we commit this sin, every other sin can happen. In fact, no other sin happens apart from breaking the first law. Every sin begins on the basis of having another god above God himself. Covetousness emerges, theft occurs, murder ensues, sexual immorality transpires, disobedient children come[5]…all as a result of breaking the first point of the law.

---

4   J. D. Greer, pastor of The Summit Church in NC, uses this fact in his blog. He references Jewish scholar Moshe Halbertal's book *Idolatry*, in which Halbertal claims that the story of the Old Testament is primarily that of the conflict between the true God and all false challengers.

5   I love this one. You have a list of what we would consider "big sins" followed by the simply stated, yet difficult, command to honor our father and mother.

Idolatry is always the reason we ever do anything wrong. It is what John Calvin argued was the fundamental motivation behind all law-breaking. It is the personal declaration of value given to my selfish desires, my selfish intentions, my self-serving ideas above God. I don't believe there is any irony that we see proof of this even as God was giving the command against idolatry. Remember the Israelites at Mount Sinai? As God was graciously giving Moses the Law, they were crafting a golden calf to worship. Their self-centeredness demanded something they could ascribe value to. They took the gifts God granted them during their rescue from Egypt and crafted an idol to worship.

Most would understand and agree that idols fail to bring lasting satisfaction. All idols ultimately disappoint us and enslave us. This book isn't meant to be an argument merely against idolatry. Instead, I want to turn our attention to the complexity of idolatry as it specifically relates to grace. It's one thing to know the concept of idolatry, but it's completely different to know how convoluted it is and how deep it goes in our view of grace.

THE GRACIOUS JOURNEY OF IDOLATRY

Now you're probably asking, "Dave, what does this have to do with grace? And where did you come to the conclusion that grace can be an idol?" Well, let me tell you where this notion started. This thought began when my oldest son, David, was about four years old. At that age and in that season, Thomas the Tank Engine was a tremendously big deal. From the TV show to the videos, David absolutely loved all things Thomas. He also loved collecting all the wooden train characters from the series. If you remember, they were the ones with the faces on them. There was Thomas, Lucy, Percy, Toby, and Gordon, just to name a few. Even to this day, we've kept many of these items, hoping that their popularity will make them worth something one day...of course, they are probably only worth our own memories.

Well, one Christmas stands out vividly. My wife and I decided to get him a Thomas the Tank Engine train table. But it wasn't just any old train table; it was the table of all tables (did I mention that he was our first of four sons?). It was one of those train tables you had to build from scratch and the tracks could be customized to whatever layout you wanted. This would allow the trains to be played with from the perfect height. So that Christmas Eve, we put our sons to bed early so that we could have ample time to build this train table, with the hope that on Christmas morning our son would be blown away by the magnitude of this phenomenal gift. Every parent knows the beauty and joy of that moment. I wanted it to be absolutely perfect. Not only the table put together, but also the tracks arranged in some elaborate formation with every type of mountain and tunnel imaginable.

So I began to build the train table at about 9:00 p.m. that Christmas Eve. Truth be told, I'm not the handiest guy in the world…9:00 easily became 11:00, 11:00 eventually became midnight. Motivated by the overwhelming joy that would be experienced by my son in the morning, I finally finished at 3:30 in the morning. I was absolutely exhausted, but there was no denying that this was one of the best Thomas the Tank Engine train tables ever assembled in the entire world.[6] I went to bed.

Of course, my son was young, he was excited, and so he woke up early, running into our bedroom yelling, "Hey, Mom and Dad, it's Christmas morning!" And we ran down the steps with great excitement to see his reaction to the surprise that awaited. As soon as he entered the room and saw the train table, as if on cue, he let out a squeal of excitement. He made his way over to the train table to begin to play with his newfound gift. Of course, I was right by his side. I said, "Hey, buddy…let me show you something," and I began to demonstrate how the train moved up the mountain and how he could guide the train through the tunnel. My tender leading was stopped as he looked at me and said, "No, Daddy, it's mine! Don't you touch it!" And he pushed my hands away as if I was trespassing on some stranger's property.

---

6   Slight exaggeration!

Now mind you, I'd been up most of the night building this *for him*. At this point there are two options. I'm returning the train table to the store (which is a viable option, considering the state of my exhaustion) or squeezing out any mercy and grace that I can for having slept three hours the night before. I, of course, remembered that it was Christmas morning, and I decided mercy and grace was on the agenda for the day. But what I remember most in the moment is stepping back and pondering what had just taken place. Now I know he's four years old and I completely understand his excitement, but I couldn't help but think: "Do you not get it...I was the one who bought this gift for you...I was the one who labored over this...I was the one who built it, stressed over it, prepared it, and gave it to you. And this is what you come back with? 'It's mine'? Listen, it's anything but yours!" As you can probably tell, I'm still going to counseling over this moment.

THE DISTORTION OF GRACE

WHEN WE TAKE WHAT GOD has graciously given, and we say, "It's mine!" This is exactly where all idolatry begins. Where all sin begins. It begins with a distortion of grace. The gift becomes greater than the gift-giver.

I want to show you how this looks from the very beginning of our story. From the first pages of Scripture, we see this glaring in our face. In Genesis 1:26 we have the sixth day of creation. God had just created the earth and now he turns his attention to the prize of his creation, man. Verses 26–27 say: "Then God said, 'Let us make man in our image, after our likeness. And let them have dominion over the fish of the sea and over the birds of the heavens and over the livestock and over all the earth and over every creeping thing that creeps on the earth.' So God created man in his own image, in the image of God he created him; male and female he created them." We come to verse 28: "And God blessed them. And God said to them, 'Be fruitful and multiply and fill the earth and subdue it, and have dominion over the fish of the sea and over the birds of the heavens and over every living thing that moves on the earth.' And God said, 'Behold, I have given you every plant yielding seed that is on the face of all the earth, and every tree with seed in its fruit.'" And at the end of that sixth and final day God says, "It is very good." This is the only place in creation where he says, "It is very good."

Look again at Genesis 1:28. It says, "God blessed them." In Hebrew, this word is בָּרַךְ, *barak*. Now don't get political with me. Some of you conspiracy theorists just all of a sudden went, "Ahhhhh, is that right?" This has no connection to our former president. This is an absolutely beautiful Hebrew word, *barak*, and in its basic form it means, "to bless, to kneel or to prosper." In this statement we see the first act of the grace of God. God blesses Adam and Eve. God gives them dominion...God prospers them. It is important to note that grace was given and demonstrated well before the fall ever happened. Peter reminds us in 1 Peter 1:20 that God knew before the foundation of the world that Christ would go to the cross. That means that God still gave them life, even though they didn't deserve it, still gave them dominion even though they would lose it, and still blessed them even though he knew what would happen. If there is grace, this must be it.

Genesis 2 is actually a restatement of chapter 1, with a bit more details. But in chapter 2 we see another aspect of God's grace revealed. Genesis 2:15–17 says, "The Lord God took the man and put him in the garden of Eden to work it and keep it. And the Lord God commanded the man, saying, 'You may surely eat of every tree of the garden, but of the tree of the knowledge of good and evil you shall not eat, for in the day that you eat of it you shall surely die.'" After giving them the gift of dominion over creation, God follows with what I would call the gift of warning. Notice those two things. He says, "I give you dominion, I give everything to you as a gift...the birds, the fish, the animals, they're all yours. This is your place, have dominion." And now God warns them, "I give you all the trees of the garden but one—don't eat it." The gracious gift of blessing followed by the gracious gift of warning. We don't naturally connect a warning with a gracious act—until disaster strikes. How important a gracious warning becomes when you know it's going to protect what matters most. A good warning becomes just as important to life as a great blessing.

Interestingly, this is true all throughout the Bible. These two gracious acts. Whenever you find the idea of grace, it always comes in those two forms. God gives and God warns. Remember Noah? He says, "Noah, I want you to build an ark." God blesses him and says, "I'm going to keep you from the rain, the flood. But this also served as a warning to others. For almost 1,000 years, God had been warning about this moment. In fact, Enoch named his son Methuselah, which means, "When he is dead, judgment will come." Of course, Methuselah was Noah's grandfather and the longest living person in history. It can be safely assumed that Noah picked up this same message of warning as he was building the ark. Of course for Noah, the message would have been all the more imminent. The New Testament seems to confirm this by describing Noah as a "preacher of righteousness" (2 Peter 2:5). It seems logical that God gave Noah and the people both a blessing and a warning—blessing through the provision of the ark and warning by making Noah a "preacher of righteousness" over the 120 years he spent building the ark.

Remember Israel? He says, "I'm going to give you this land I promised to Abraham. I'm going to let you conquer this land, but don't give in to the pagan cultures, don't give in to the foreigners that will tempt you in the land. Be careful with them because they're idol worshippers." He blesses them with the land, but he also warns them of what could happen if they compromise. And then we have Jesus. Jesus comes on the scene and says, "I've come to give you life, and to give it to you abundantly." He blesses, but he also warns, "But I warn you, judgment will come." I would go so far as to argue that whenever you see the concept of grace throughout the Bible, it always comes in those two forms. It comes in blessing and in warning. And Genesis gives us this two-fold picture of God's grace from the very beginning.

These two perspectives shouldn't surprise us. If you're a parent, you know this to be true...it's exactly how grace is demonstrated to our own kids. We bless them with a house and clothing and food, and eventually we give them dominion over certain things and encourage them to live on their own. And we bless them. But we also warn them… "Hey, you better not do this," or "You better remember this in life." And sometimes we're warning them even more than blessing them… "Why do you keep doing this? Don't you know I said not to do that?" That's the picture of grace. God gives them dominion; God gives them warning and says, "Now go enjoy it. Go live it up." He gives them everything to enjoy fully and freely, and then puts a fence around them so they will continue enjoying his gifts without fear of consequence. Why do we put fences around our yards? It's not so our kids will live in fear, but so they will play with unhindered freedom in the safe confines of the home. It's undeserved, it's unmerited, and it's unearned. This means that grace isn't merely a word that's meant to be explained, it's an experience meant to be lived. A grace-filled and grace-protected experience we're meant to live out…and that's exactly the point. These two ideas are where we get our definition for the word *grace*. A definition that we will return to as we unpack how grace becomes idolatrous.

> **Grace is the unmerited, undeserved, and unearned gifts of God.**[7]

Adam and Eve did not earn, merit, or deserve what God had just given them. He made them with the ability to have righteous dominion, but they didn't deserve it. Even knowing what was about to come, he graciously gave it to them anyway. And to demonstrate his grace all the more, he warns them. He warns them of the consequence of taking the gift and twisting it, of misaligning it. And if you know the story, you quickly find grace meeting idolatry.

No doubt, Genesis 3 gives us the answer to many of life's deepest questions. It also reveals to us the initiation of idolatrous grace.

---

7   You will notice the word *gifts* in the plural form. As we will see, grace is more than a momentary act…more than a definite point. For every gracious act of God, there is a domino effect of gifts that follow.

Genesis 3:1–7 describes this moment: "Now the serpent was more crafty than any other beast of the field that the Lord God had made. He said to the woman, 'Did God actually say, "You shall not eat of any tree in the garden"?' And the woman said to the serpent, 'We may eat of the fruit of the trees in the garden, but God said, "You shall not eat of the fruit of the tree that is in the midst of the garden, neither shall you touch it, lest you die."'[8] But the serpent said to the woman, 'You will not surely die. For God knows that when you eat of it your eyes will be opened, and you will be like God, knowing good and evil.' So when the woman saw that the tree was good for food, and that it was a delight to the eyes, and that the tree was to be desired to make one wise, she took of its fruit and ate, and she also gave some to her husband who was with her, and he ate. Then the eyes of both were opened, and they knew that they were naked."

This is what scholars call the fall, the moment that sin came into the world. We continue to experience the magnitude of this choice to this day. But what stands out in this passage is what is described in Genesis 3:6. It says that the woman saw "the tree was to be desired to make one wise." What's interesting is that this is not the word *wisdom*. The word here is the Hebrew word לָכַשׂ, *sakal*. It literally means "understanding, attractiveness, prosperity, and success." Now why does that matter? It's actually a synonym of the Hebrew word *barak* that we just discussed. These terms are used interchangeably throughout the Scripture to describe moments of blessing or success. Eve saw the potential that she could be better blessed, more prosperous, and have greater success if she ate the fruit.

Do you see what she just did? She took the grace of God and she exchanged it. She manipulated it. She chose the dark side...the shadow side. And she said, "Oh, wait, God said not to eat; God was gracious in giving me every other tree, a million other trees in the garden,

---

8   It is interesting to note that Eve makes a law in her description to the serpent. God says, "Don't eat." She describes it as "Don't touch." Whether this was Eve's commentary on God's command and warning or a collaboration of Adam and Eve together, it's interesting that law is introduced so quickly in our story.

but this one he warned me about." Unfortunately, she gets caught in the web of the serpent's deception, which leads her to a heartbreaking conclusion. "It looks like I'm missing something. It seems like there's more opportunity, more success, more grace. There's something greater in that fruit," and she takes it, eats it, and sin happens. You know what's remarkable? That is exactly how sin happens in every one of our lives. Grace meets idolatry and sin results. Ironically, that same story that happened thousands of years ago…still happens today. That story is our story of sin and it can be defined in a simple equation:

> **Grace (the gift of God)**
> **+**
> **Idolatry (the gift becomes greater than the Gift-Giver)**
> **= Sin (always)**

Sin happens when we take the gift of God, whether a blessing or warning, and allow it to become bigger than God himself. We exchange the gracious gift for what it was never meant to be: an idol. Every sin stems from warping God's gifts of blessing or warning. Think about any sin you have committed. It begins as a gift exchanged. We distort it; we twist it for our selfish desires, our self-assurances, and our self-serving intentions. And that is how grace becomes an idol.

CHAPTER TWO

GRACE-BASED IDOLS

B ELIEVE IT OR NOT, THE subtle twist of grace shows up constantly in our lives. When we think of sin, we naturally think of some horrifically bad thing that we have done or are doing. But it shows up much more imperceptibly. No one wakes up one day and says, "I have an idol." Instead, idols demonstrate themselves in our everyday life in a much more delicate and deceiving way. We probably don't notice initially, but eventually we will see their evidence in two predominant forms…visible and invisible.

VISIBLE GRACE-BASED IDOLS

THE FIRST IS WHAT I would call visible grace-based idols. These are obvious gifts that God has given to us for our enjoyment and his glory that become twisted in the web of idolatry. These are usually easily recognizable and outward. Let me give you some examples and expound on a few. Consider marriage. Didn't God give us the gift of marriage? It's the first institution given by God as a gift of his grace to humanity. It's meant to be a reflection of his glory and a lifelong journey filled with the joy of marriage bliss. But what happens? Our idol hearts twist it and eventually marriage becomes an attempt to gain personal satisfaction through our spouse. We say things like, "My spouse ought to do this for me and that for me." Instead of our marriage being filled with "I do's" it's filled with "I expect." We unknowingly try to find our identity in who they are and what they do for us. And what ends up happening? Dissatisfaction. Frustration. Anger. Sin. A graciously given gift becomes an idol.

Let's take our kids, for example. If you're a parent, you know exactly where this is headed. In fact, I could hear a slight snicker as you read this. God gives us the gifts of our children and what do we do? Either we make them the most prominent blessing of life or we view them as the largest burden we carry. Probably for most of us, our kids have been viewed in both ways depending on the season. We make them an idol. We begin to find our identity in who our kids are or aren't, which consequently leads to selfish parenting. Our kids become an instrument we use to define us instead of the calling we have to help them to be solely defined by God. All of a sudden, what happens? Sin…persists.

Consider money. God gives us the gift of financial resources, but what do we do? We take the gift and we twist it and we say, "I need more! I want more!" And we begin to hold on to things with greed. How about self-image? However broken we may feel, God gave us these bodies and these features. Yet the pressure of our fallen world convinces us that we aren't enough. So we look to find our self-image and self-confidence in something else. Or on the flip side, we read that God tells us to take care of these physical "temples" that he has given to us. But what happens? We take the grace of God, our bodies, and we begin to distort it and say, "Man, I'm not enough. I've got to look better, and I have to start this diet,"[1] and what happens? We twist it and we begin to find our identity merely in how we look instead of who we are as followers of Christ.

And of course, we can't forget about the subject of sex. Is it not God who first gave us sex as a gift for procreation and enjoyment? And what do we do? We take the gracious gift of God and we twist it, we exchange it, and what happens? We make it an idol, and the next thing you know…sin abounds. The list could go on and on with things like desires, substances, even God's law lived through a life of legalism… everything we have been given visibly as a gift from God can be bent toward our pursuits. God's visible grace can become an evident idol.

---

1   This is not saying that there is anything wrong with looking better or dieting. But the number of diet plans in our culture alone proves how dieting can easily become part of our identity.

INVISIBLE GRACE-BASED IDOLS

JUST AS THERE ARE VISIBLE grace-based idols, we also find what I would call invisible grace-based idols. These are more intrinsic qualities or virtues that have been graciously given by God, but just like their counterparts, get twisted in the trap of idolatry. Take for example power. God graciously gives us, the prize of his creation, dominion and influence. Yet we take what God has given and say, "No, no, no…I'm going to do it on my own. I'll do it. I'll bear it. I'll handle it. I've got this. God, let me take the reins…I've got this thing figured out." Instead of "Jesus take the wheel" it's "Jesus, I've got the wheel!" And we take the grace of God found in dominion and influence, and we distort it for our selfish desires.

Or how about control? God gives us control over things in our lives, and what happens? In a world with great uncertainty, we attempt to control the world around us. We take the concept of control and we twist it. We begin to micromanage life, and the next thing you know, anger and manipulation abounds. Consider purpose. Of course, we believe that God is the ultimate fulfiller of our purpose, but we begin to think greater purpose might come through our careers, our financial situations, even our relationships. What happens? We attempt to claw our way to the top only to find sin waiting to trap us. Of course, we can't forget comfort. As Christians, we know that we can only find comfort in God, and God alone, but how many of us are uncomfortable, to the point that we're searching everywhere else for comfort? We are worshippers of comfort who eventually begin to see the things in our lives as either potential comforters or obstacles of our comfort. What happens? We distort the gracious gift of comfort and we find comfort in substances, in relationships, in work, in money, and many other things. We pursue or we push away things that we believe will inhibit our comfort. Obviously, there are a myriad of other examples, which are internal and unseen, yet just as real and just as dangerous.

This naturally leads to an important question: How does this take place? How does grace get twisted and God's gracious gifts become idols? We find the answer given in Paul's words to the Romans. Paul writes in Romans 1:18–21,

> *For the wrath of God is revealed from heaven against all ungodliness and unrighteousness of men, who by their unrighteousness suppress the truth. For what can be known about God is plain to them, because God has shown it to them. For his invisible attributes, namely, his eternal power and divine nature, have been clearly perceived, ever since the creation of the world, in the things that have been made. So they are without excuse. For although they knew God, they did not honor him as God or give thanks to him, but they became futile in their thinking, and their foolish hearts were darkened.*

This is not only a description of the pagan Roman culture specifically, and the first-century world generally, but also a report of all men and women without Christ. Notice carefully what it says...it declares that we all know God. Now this might sound a little weird if you claim that you don't know God. But Paul writes that God has revealed himself to us whether we accept it or not. First, God reveals himself through creation. Creation screams the glory of God. But we also can clearly observe God's invisible attributes. His grace, mercy, and his love are evident. So what's the big problem? Paul says the problem isn't that the attributes are hidden. In fact, they're not even locked up waiting for us to find them. The problem is that we actually don't acknowledge them and honor God because of them. We don't give him thanks.

Isn't it interesting that he uses the words *honor* and *thanksgiving*? Here is a God who has demonstrated himself, an everlasting God who has given us the eternal gift of himself. And Paul writes that we do not honor him and we do not thank him. Imagine receiving a phenomenal gift from a generous donor...a car, a vacation, or a million dollars. You would certainly send a big thank you...probably the best Hallmark card you could find...maybe even dinner on you. But Paul is saying we don't take the gift and come back to God with a grander view of his goodness, a heart overflowing with thanks and honor. No, instead, we take the gift that God gives and say, "God, thank you for my life…thank you for creation, and now I'm going to go live life on my own and for my own." We twist it. We abuse it. We distort it. Grace + idolatry = sin.

But let's take this one step further. What does the process of this distortion of grace look like? Paul doesn't leave us answerless. He continues setting the tone of the letter in Romans 1:25, "Because they exchanged the truth about God for a lie and worshiped and served the creature rather than the Creator…" See it there? We take the truth of God, the grace of God, especially God's revelation of Himself, and we twist it and exchange it for a lie. And we serve the creation…the power, the control, the authority, the money, the sex, the relationships… whether visible or invisible, we serve the creation rather than realizing that the gracious gift of God should lead us back to the glory of the Creator. And this is the basis of all grace-based idols. And this is the source for how grace becomes an idol…

> **Grace becomes an idol when we exchange God himself for the gracious gifts that come from Him.**

Read that description again. Grace becomes an idol when we exchange God himself for his gracious gifts. We exchange God's purposes for our preferences. We exchange God's praise for our pleasures. Paul beautifully outlines the horrific exchange that happens in the human heart. We say, "Forget you, God. We don't believe you're glorious, we don't believe that you're worthy of worship, and we don't believe that your all-surpassing beauty is satisfying to our hearts. What is satisfying to our hearts is this person or this thing that you have made. We'll take your gift…but in our way."

Let me ask you this heartfelt question, a question that will direct the conversation over the next few pages. In what way has grace been distorted, and twisted in your life, and now has caused the gifts of God to become an idol? How have you relegated grace from the action of God to simply the knowledge of God? In what ways have you demoted grace from the motivation of your life to merely a theological word with little impact? John, the disciple, warns us of this in his first epistle.

> We know that we are from God, and the whole world lies in the power of the evil one. And we know that the Son of God has come and has given us understanding, so that we may know him who is true; and we are in him who is true, in his Son Jesus Christ. He is the true God and eternal life. Little children, keep yourselves from idols. (1 John 5:19–21)

Here it is again. A beautiful description followed by a gracious warning. He says you know God is true, you know that life is in him. Every good and perfect gift is from the Father of Lights and the God of Glory. Now, little children, be careful of idols. Notice the fatherly warning. The potential of idols is a real danger to your journey with Christ. So what do I do if I've made idols out of God's grace, if I've taken the grace of God—the gift of God—and exchanged it for a lie?

1. **Identify the idol.** What is your idol? Is it visible? Is your idol what your spouse thinks about you? Is your idol in the identity and value you receive from friends or coworkers? Is your idol in the obedience of your children? Is your idol in money? Work? Success? Sex? Or is it invisible? Is it power? Control? Purpose? Image? What is your idol? An easy way to determine what your idol might be is by answering this question, "If I just had this in my life, it would be better." What is that? You have identified your potential idol.

2. **Connect the idol to the area of misaligned and misapplied grace.** What I mean by this is that I should take the idol that I have allowed to control my life, whatever that might be, and connect it back to the grace of God. If the idol originated as a gracious gift from God in the first place, I want to connect it back to what God originally desired in giving me that gift. Why do I have this desire? Where did that desire come from? If it's money, doesn't

God give me the resources to live? What does he desire me to do with my finances? If it's sex, isn't God the one who gave me the gift of sex? So what is the context in which sex should be experienced and enjoyed that brings him the most glory? So I connect it back to the grace of God. To state it another way, what am I trying to manufacture that God has already given to me in a true context of glory and enjoyment?

3. **Displace the idol with the proper perspective of God's grace, namely God himself.** By the way, notice you can't just get rid of an idol in your life.[2] You have to displace it. Rid and replace it. And as Christians we want to put Christ in its place. We put what God has offered to us in its place. You know why I say that? Because I have found in my life that every time I sin, it's because I have a small view of God. Every time I sin, it's because I view God in a small little box instead of the massive, indescribable version of who he is. It reminds me of some verses in Colossians.

> *If then you have been raised with Christ, seek the things that are above, where Christ is, seated at the right hand of God. Set your minds on things that are above, not on things that are on earth. For you have died, and your life is hidden with Christ in God. When Christ who is your life appears, then you also will appear with him in glory. Put to death therefore what is earthly in you: sexual immorality, impurity, passion, evil desire, and covetousness, which is idolatry.* (Colossians 3:1–5)

Paul says to put to death what is earthly in us. And what are these earthly characteristics? Idols. So he exhorts us to displace the idol with a proper view of Jesus. Displace the idol, not by morality, or self-discipline, or even by claiming more grace. We displace the idol by seeing the beauty and the excellency of Jesus Christ, and the gifts

---

2   I again would highly recommend Tim Keller's *Counterfeit Gods* for a deeper understanding of replacing idols.

that he has offered. We overcome the world not by having more grace. We overcome the world by realizing the grace we already have in Jesus, who satisfies our every longing. That is the gospel message. Jesus is more beautiful and more hope-giving than anything he has given. It's saying, "God, instead of this idol that I have fashioned out of your grace, I want more of you. I want to know you more, serve you more, and worship you more. And in this moment I am tempted to make an idol out of grace, I choose you instead.

Now that we have set the theological basis for grace being an idol, we can look more clearly at the dark side of grace, the many practical ways idolatrous grace plays out in our lives, and how we can restore grace to its intended purpose.

NOW WHAT?

Read: Genesis 1-3; Exodus 20:1-3; Romans 1:18-32; 1 John 5:19-21

Discuss:

1. Idolatry can have multiple meanings. Define idolatry in your own terms: In what ways do you see idolatry displayed throughout the Scripture (give some examples)? What do you make of the fact that the law begins with two commands concerning idolatry (Exodus 20 and the Ten Commandments)? How does idolatry act as the igniter of every other sin?

2. Define grace: How does God demonstrate grace in the creation story (Genesis 1-2)? What two ways are God's gracious gifts demonstrated throughout Scripture? How have you seen the gifts of blessing and warning in your own spiritual journey?

3. The fall (Genesis 3) unravels God's gracious gift of blessing and warning to Adam and Eve. Restate the equation that defines sin? Describe a few examples of how you see visible and invisible grace-based idols portrayed in your own life and in our world today.

4. Paul in Romans 1 describes the journey of twisted grace. He describes the exchange that takes place between our knowledge, glory, and gratitude of God for the gifts that he has graciously given. In what ways do we exchange His purposes for our preferences and His praise for our pleasures?

5. In what specific place in your life has grace been distorted, twisted, and misapplied and now the gift of God has become an idol for you?

Pray:

Pray that Christ would reveal to you where you have replaced God with His gracious gifts.

Memorize/Meditate:

"We know that we are from God, and the whole world lies in the power of the evil one. And we know that the Son of God has come and has given us understanding, so that we may know Him who is true; and we are in Him who is true, in His Son Jesus Christ. He is the true God and eternal life. Little children, keep yourselves from idols" (1 John 5:19-21).

CHAPTER THREE

MESSY GRACE

Are we to continue in sin that grace may abound?
By no means! (Romans 6:1–2)

I F YOU WERE TO ASK any member of my family who the messiest
person is, there would be emphatic agreement. Now I'm not referring to messy in the sense of disorganized. If you go to my office or
if you enter our home, it is well put together. Personally, I don't like
a mess. What I'm referring to is the most likely to have an accidental
messy moment. Those awkward moments when you spill your drink,
drop food, or get ketchup all over your shirt. If you were to ask anyone
in my family, especially my wife and four boys, who in our house is
the messiest when it comes to accidents, they are going to say, without
hesitation, "Dad!" And believe it or not, it's true. When we go out to
eat, I seem to always have a case of the spills. If there's ketchup on the
table, somehow I am a victim of it exploding all over the place. And
it always seems to lead to a profusely apologetic conversation with a
waiter or waitress.

This cannot be more clearly seen than what happened years
ago. My wife and I took our three-year-old son to see Barney the Musical. I can't believe I just confessed this to you. But, yes, he was into
the loving purple dinosaur and we just couldn't resist taking our son
to a live stage performance of Barney.[1] Of course, my wife dragged me
along for this surprise for my son. As a loving husband and father, I felt
it was my duty to go (at least that's how I tell the story). This was my
son's first experience seeing a show like this, so we, felt it was a special
enough moment to purchase a souvenir. At one of the intermissions,
my family and I ventured out to look at the souvenirs and buy popcorn

---

1   For Barney fans out there…it was the show *Barney's Musical Castle*. If
     you have never seen the video, I recommend it. You're welcome!

and a drink. But we couldn't settle for just any size popcorn and drink; it was a special night, so we had to get the supersize, souvenir soda (specifically for me). After getting our snacks, we made our way back to the theater seats.

This is where the story goes south. Just as the next act was about to begin, this big drink, filled to the brim with Coca-Cola, went flying out of my hands in excitement. The drink literally went everywhere. As if in a Coca-Cola water park, the folks in front of us received a nice, cold Coke bath. It was rolling like a river under our feet and the feet of all those around us. Allyson, my wife, picked up our son and dragged him out. It was so bad that some attendees were exiting the theater like it was the *Titanic* about to sink. True story. If I can confess, I truly believe I was cursed for going to see Barney. But that's for a different story.

Whatever the case, fair warning: if you are ever around me at all, especially if you go out to eat with me, I can be messy. Not intentionally...accidentally. So proceed with caution. As crazy as that sounds, similarly, there are times in life when grace is messy. In the previous chapters, we said that grace, by definition, is the unmerited, undeserved, and unearned gifts of God. And it's precisely at this point where messy grace begins. You ask, "Dave, what do you mean? Why would you say grace gets messy at this point?" Because if we're going to make the claim that grace is unmerited, undeserved, and unearned, you and I have to make some pretty bold confessions. If we say that grace is unmerited, undeserved, and unearned, what does this say about us? We make no contribution. We offer nothing to the journey. We are worthless. Let's be honest—that's not an easy truth to swallow.

Now if you were to look up the subject of grace in any theology book, namely systematic theology books, you will most likely find a distinct section on grace and a separate section on sin. They are almost always divided. Now there are many good reasons why this is so. But I believe one simple reason is that we, by nature, don't want the beautiful concept of grace to be mixed with the despair of sin. Who would want to mar the splendor of the grace of God with the topic of our deepest mess? This would even be true in a world where the topic of sin is becoming increasingly unpopular. More and more, we don't like to talk about sin. In fact, to dialogue about sin, and especially to preach against sin, has become increasingly out of style. It's as if the topic of sin is a ferociously offensive topic. As a result, you rarely find grace and sin together anymore. But can I confess something to you? In the real world and in the context of Scripture, we find that sin and grace actually go hand in hand. Over and over again throughout the Bible, you see them uniquely linked. And the reason is clear. It's impossible to appreciate grace without an understanding of sin. Because grace is a subject found at the heart of sin. And it can be quite messy.

THE MAGNITUDE OF OUR MESS

I CAN IMAGINE WE WOULD all agree, if we are being honest, that most Christians, in fact most people, don't feel as bad as they actually are. We have a hard time admitting the depth of our own sin. We are accustomed to cleaning up messes. We are taught from an early age to clean up what we mess up. Pick up after yourself. But sin is a mess we can't clean up. I've heard people say, "I've sinned but I haven't sin-sinned! I'm not that bad!" Of course, that's a declaration of comparison. And you know, it's probably true. We aren't that bad, especially if you compare your life to the ones observed on some reality TV shows. Have you watched any criminal reality shows lately? Wow…there are some pretty crazy characters out there. Most of us aren't even close.[2] In fact, we can all find someone who is worse than us…someone who can make us feel better about ourselves.

But I want to show you what Scripture actually says about us. In Romans 5, we see the topics of grace and sin described together.[3]

---

2   I do think this is a self-evident point. The fact that we compare ourselves to others proves our sinfulness. Specifically, the sin of pride.

3   Romans 5 has been called one of the most difficult passages in the New Testament to translate and understand. The reason seems to be based upon the fact that the comparisons Paul is using don't exactly run parallel.

Therefore, just as sin came into the world through one man, and death through sin, and so death spread to all men because all sinned— for sin indeed was in the world before the law was given, but sin is not counted where there is no law. Yet death reigned from Adam to Moses, even over those whose sinning was not like the transgression of Adam, who was a type of the one who was to come. (Romans 5:12-14)

In verses 12–14, Paul makes a bold argument to demonstrate the worthiness of the gospel. He reminds us that the gospel begins with sin. When you consider the Jewish audience in the city of Rome, what he describes could be considered shocking. He tells them that sin came through Adam and passed to all. Now there are two predominant points that Paul is attempting to make. The first one is that sin preempted the Law of Moses. Sin actually occurred well before the Law was given. Consequently, you don't need a law to have sin. And as if that wasn't enough, he takes it one step further by describing how the law actually reveals our sin. Specifically, the law shows us how far we have missed the mark and it demonstrates the deep need we have for Christ. Law or no law, Jew or Gentile, sin has passed from one man, Adam, to everybody. And that is not a small detail. As the Bible talks about sin, an illustration permeates its understanding. It uses an analogy of a sickness or virus that gets passed from one to the next. It's the idea that we have this inherited sin that came from Adam.

By the way, the words found in Romans 5 were exactly what led church father Augustine to discover and describe what he called original sin. He articulated the idea that when Adam sinned, the fallen nature, the old sin nature, was now automatically passed down through conception to every single person. This concept is more fully confirmed at the end of verse 12, "so death to all men." Why? "Because all sinned." Death comes because all sin.

Undoubtedly, this isn't a new argument that Paul is making. If you turn back just two chapters, Paul had already declared, "None is righteous, no, not one; no one understands; no one seeks for God. All have turned aside; together they have become worthless; no one does good, not even one" (Romans 3:10–12).[4] This means that every person, every child, and every baby has sinned. Paul repeats this idea a few verses later, "All have sinned and fall short of the glory of God" (Romans 3:23). No one can say, "We aren't affected! We don't have a mess! We are clean!" In the theology world, this is what we call the doctrine of depravity. I know this is deep. But it's an important doctrine, and we're going to see its connection to grace in a moment, so bear with me. Depravity can be defined as...

> **Our sinful corruption, as a result of man's fall and its effect on the entire human race, is so great and so immense that we are natural-born slaves of sin, spiritually dead, and morally unable to overcome our own rebellion and blindness.**

Now let me explain this in simpler terms. Notice the three main points of this definition. As a result of our sinfulness, we are natural-born slaves of sin, we are spiritually dead, and we are morally unable to overcome it. All of these are highlighted throughout the Scripture.

NATURAL-BORN SLAVES OF SIN

WE ARE NATURAL-BORN SLAVES OF sin. In John 8:34 it says, "Jesus answered them, 'Truly, truly, I say to you, everyone who practices sin is a slave to sin.'" So if we're born with sin, then guess what...we're slaves to it. This is repeated over and over again in the Scripture. We're bound to it, it's who we are, and it's our nature at birth. I would take this one step further and argue that we all feel the weight of our slavery to sin. Have you ever struggled to overcome something and found it difficult? Maybe it's a habit, an unhealthy relationship, or an inappropriate reaction. Why is it such a struggle? Because we are slaves to sin.

---

4   These verses include quotes of Psalm 14 and 53. Paul is intentionally using the Old Testament to prove sinfulness.

SPIRITUALLY DEAD

WE ARE ALSO SPIRITUALLY DEAD. Ephesians chapter 2 describes our spiritual death. It says, "And you were dead in the trespasses and sins in which you once walked, following the course of this world, following the prince of the power of the air..." (Ephesians 2:1–2). We are unequivocally dead in our sinfulness. It reminds me of the previous number one show on TV, *The Walking Dead*. If you have never seen it, it's basically a zombie-focused TV drama (although fans deny it's all about zombies). This passage describes us this way. We are the walking dead. Yes, we are physically alive, but we are spiritually dead.

MORALLY UNABLE

ALL THROUGH THE SCRIPTURE, WE see that there is nothing we can add and no work that can be done to fix our situation. There is no power in us to clean up our mess. In fact, the more we try to overcome our sinfulness, to wipe away the mess, the more likely we are to continue in sin and potentially make our mess even greater. It's like attempting to wash paint off your hands with no soap...all it does is spread the mess.

Before we describe the implications of total depravity specifically as it relates to grace, it's immensely important for us to understand what this doctrine is not. Total depravity doesn't mean that there's no sense of right or wrong in us as humans. In fact, C. S. Lewis described it as "an ought" inside of all of us.[5] Built in us is the idea of right and wrong, the idea of what is good and not. We all have this basic idea of goodness. God has put that into us. Additionally, this doesn't mean that every sinner is devoid of good qualities that are going to help society. We've all met people who don't know Christ that are great people and have qualities that are beneficial for mankind. Total depravity also doesn't mean that we struggle with every sin. Hopefully, there are sins that we haven't committed nor desire to commit (like murder).

The problem is, even our good deeds are actually sinful? Even when we are doing something good, we ironically are actually attempt-

---

5   C. S. Lewis, *Mere Christianity* (1952; repr., San Francisco: Harper, 2001), 16–18.

ing to make ourselves feel better. Isaiah 64 describes our good deeds as messy rags. Why? Because we are doing them with self-centered motivation. We're doing them because it enhances our feelings concerning our situation. Even though we probably wouldn't easily admit it, when we do good, we are making ourselves feel better about life. Depravity tells us we are a mess and there is no possibility to fix ourselves. And the Scripture reveals over and over again that the mess is bad and has the potential to be worse.

Now, I'm sure by now you are asking, "Okay, I get the depth of my mess—can you please stop depressing me? I mean, what's the point? Where are you going with this?" The point...the reason the gospel begins with it, Paul addresses it, and we should consider it is because we battle this sickness every day...we face this mess, and it's impossible to deny.

This reminds me of an unforgettable lesson I learned a few years ago. I don't know how you are, but I go at life pretty hard. I work hard. I play hard. I don't know if there is any correlation, but I don't get sick all that often. I'd like to think that I only get sick if I slow down. In fact, I would go so far as to say that I refuse to get sick. That sounds like a weird statement, but I like to think that I can mentally beat sickness.

A few years ago, we had the flu running through our family. All four of our boys had it badly. We were right in the middle of a busy season, balancing many different family and ministry obligations. So I pulled my wife aside and gave her a pep talk. And I said to her, "Baby-love (that's my pet name for her), we can't get sick. We've got to tell ourselves we're not getting sick." And she gave me this mysterious look like I've lost my mind and said, "Dave, can you actually do that? Can you actually tell yourself not to get sick? Do you believe that's all it takes?" Now I have to admit, she was being overly sarcastic in her questioning. Needless to say I responded confidently, "Maybe you can't...but I can!"

Well guess what happened—she got sick a day later (surprise!). And I lovingly said to her, "I told you, didn't I. You didn't fight it!" (In a small, unspoken way, I questioned her faith). Well, a week later, I ate my words. Not only did I get sick, I got sick-sick. I was down-and-out for a week and a half. It was miserable and I was humbled. To say I "ate crow" would be an understatement.[6] That's exactly the point I am attempting to demonstrate. In Romans 3, no one is righteous. In chapter 5, sin has passed to all of us. We are all sick…we all have messes. And without first grasping sin's reality, we cannot grasp grace. We can only view true grace from the perspective of great need. That's why we need Christ. And that's exactly where we meet messy grace.

WHERE GRACE MEETS OUR MESS

OUR SIN MEETS GOD'S GRACE at this meticulous point. If you continue reading Romans 5, you see multiple words repeated. In biblical exposition, repetition can point to importance. In just a few short verses, the word *one* is repeated twelve times. The word *all* occurs eight times. But none more than the words *grace* and *gift*.[7] Paul says, "You've been given a gift, you've been given grace…and you've been overwhelmed by it." This biblical theme of grace is only more solidified when you realize that it shows up one hundred and fifty-five times in the New Testament. Over a hundred of them are in the writings of Paul, and over one-fourth of them are found in the book of Romans (twenty-four), and of those, the majority of them are found neatly in chapter 5. And you know what's even more interesting…it's found in a passage about the existence and extent of our sin. Sin is overwhelming and certainly messy…but there is grace, a gift, at the heart of it all.

While certainly true, it's still incomplete. It's not enough to merely say that grace is found at the heart of sin. This entire passage comes to a climax at Romans 5:20. It could be considered the summary statement of the passage. "Now the law came in to increase the trespass, but where sin increased, grace abounded all the more." Notice

---

6　Obviously, this should not be taken literally. Actually, eating crow would probably make you sick anyway. I couldn't eat anything. What a weird way to describe being humbled.

7　Gift and grace actually both come from the Greek word *charis*.

the words *increased* and *abounded*. Surprisingly, they are synonyms. Paul is using a play on words to make his final point of this section, but he does so uniquely, by making up his own word in the second half of the statement. The first word, *increased*, has the idea of abounding and expanding with the passing of time.

The second word is especially rare. It's only used in this passage in this way. He takes another word for *abound* and adds *hyper* to the front of it. Now if you have kids, the word *hyper* might be a common term in your house. Or maybe you are married to someone like me. My wife will sometimes say, "Dave, you're so hyper." Paul literally says sin excels but grace "hyper" excels. Grace hyper-excelled, grace hyper-increased, grace goes beyond where sin can actually go. This means that where sin adds to our lives, grace multiplies in our lives. Here is the point: grace isn't just found in the midst of sin, grace is greater than sin. Not to overstate it, but we could actually say that grace is greater than anything you put in front of it.[8] Whatever sin you place on the other side of the equation of grace, grace is greater. Whatever your regret is in your life, grace is greater. Whatever you wish never happened in your life, grace is greater. There is nothing greater than the greatness of the hyper-extended grace that God offers to us. It is the antidote to our infection…the hand of Christ wiping away our mess.

I hope the words you just read are both a beautiful description of grace and a beautiful picture of our rescue. But I have to be honest with you— it still doesn't go far enough. It's not wrong…but it still falls slightly short. See, the previous description is as far as most people go in their description of the gospel message. Grace has come to rescue us from the mess of our sin. Period. But is that all it is? It's beautiful, but still an incomplete picture. And it misses the immensity of the gospel. It's like climbing a twelve-hundred-foot high mountain and calling it the Grand Canyon. It's certainly beautiful, but it's not the Grand Canyon. It's like seeing a ripple in a lake and thinking it's a wave. It falls

---

8   A great book on this perspective of grace is Kyle Idleman's *Grace Is Greater: God's Plan to Overcome Your Past, Redeem Your Pain, and Rewrite Your Story*. I highly recommend it.

short. While it would seem that the focus of Romans 5 is grace, it's actually even more beautiful than that.

Don't miss this. Romans 5 isn't actually telling us that grace is the antidote to our sickness or the hand that cleans up the mess of our sin…it's telling us that Jesus is. Grace isn't the subject of the text… grace is the object and we are the recipients. It's the instrument used to deliver forgiveness and renewed life to us from Jesus Christ himself. To continue the sickness analogy, grace is more like the pill container that holds the pill of life that's found in Christ. It's the Shamwow[9] in the hand of Christ wiping away our messes. This is exactly the argument Paul is making in Romans. Just as sin came through Adam, and was carried to us through conception, grace is the womb that delivers us forgiveness and life in Jesus Christ.

Grace only becomes amazing, powerful, and overwhelming when it is brought to us by the authority of Christ. Only Christ can give to us grace that superabounds…a grace that tips the scales of balance on sin. Grace in the hand of Christ doesn't contain a "but." It's unconditional, it's uncontrollable, it's unpredictable, it's undomesticated, or else it's not Christ's grace—it's just our own version of grace. As I've heard one pastor describe it, "Grace is wild. Grace unsettles everything. Grace overflows the banks. Grace messes up your hair. Grace is not tame." Why? Because it's God's grace. Not *just* grace. And the argument of Romans is that by God's grace we become two-volume people. The first volume of our life is in Adam. A volume packed with the mess of our sin. But when we come to know Christ, there is a second volume, renewed life in Christ, the second perfect Adam. We deserve reproach and disapproval from Christ. But then comes the unmerited, undeserved, and unearned gift of God…grace. And grace overwhelmingly delivers. Now, that's beautiful…because that's the gospel.

So how in the world can this be considered messy grace? This chapter has focused on the mess of sin and the beauty of grace. Here

---

9   Everybody probably remembers the Shamwow infomercial. It claimed to be a cleaning towel that promised to soak up twenty times its weight in spilled liquids. It was one of the highest-grossing infomercials in the history of infomercials.

is where the struggle lies. If our story of grace stopped right there, you and I would be in heaven. If the story ended with grace delivering to us our new life in Christ, then you and I have no need for life here, and Romans would end at chapter 5. But this beautiful picture of grace I have attempted to paint doesn't stop there. There is another side of grace. It's the dark, twisted, shadow side of grace. An undesired and under-articulated side of the grace we have been offered…a messy side. Paul's description of the beautiful grace of God is immediately followed with a warning about the difficulty we can have with his grace.[10] He moves from the great blessing of grace to a warning in Romans 6. Remember in the previous chapters, I explained that grace is found both in blessing and in warning? We see it here. Paul is showing us both sides of grace, the beautiful and the messy side.

Paul begins chapter 6 with three questions and a strong declaration. "What shall we say then? Are we to continue in sin that grace may abound? By no means! How can we who died to sin still live in it?" (Romans 6:1–2). In chapter 5, Paul focused on grace. In fact, you could say chapter 5 was "all about that grace!"[11] He comes to chapter 6 and says, "Oh, I know how most people will think. If grace superabounds when sin happens, and I've got grace, why don't I just go ahead and sin? What does it matter? I've got grace! I'm not under the law, I'm under grace! I mean, God knows this is who I am. So why not go ahead and give in? Besides, grace will only continue to abound." Remarkably, the Scripture knows us better than we know ourselves.[12] And this is exactly when the beautiful grace of God becomes a messy idol. Wait, how does grace become an idol? Here it is. Grace becomes an idol when we use it to sin instead of surrender. When we use the grace meant to deliver us from sin to actually live in sin. That's the point of this entire chapter. We take the grace of God and use it our own way. Let me put this in a simple sentence:

---

10   As you most likely are aware, the chapters and verse divisions found in the Scripture weren't in the original. That's a delineation to assist us.

11   Okay! I confess…that was a bit corny. But you get the point.

12   By the way, a little side note…it's interesting that sin always seeks to use that which is good to promote evil. It's true. Sin seems to always play this subtle trick.

> **Grace becomes an idol when we use grace as an excuse for sin instead of an invitation for surrender.**

GRACE AS AN EXCUSE

I HAVE TO CONFESS, IN my position as a pastor, I have heard this ideology spoken from the mouths of many believers. I even hear it in myself. Sometimes pridefully, sometimes more passively-nonetheless it's there. Let me give you some examples.

I CAN'T HELP IT! GRACE GIVES PERMISSION.

WE SAY THINGS LIKE "I can't help it." Have you ever said that before? "I just can't help it." "God knows I'm not perfect! He can't expect me to have it all together." Or better yet, have you ever seen those bumper stickers that say, "Christians aren't perfect, they're just forgiven"? You know what's interesting about that message, the beginning is true… we aren't perfect. But we're not just forgiven. Although unintentional, isn't that last part an excuse? An excuse that says, "I'm not perfect, so God expects me to mess up sometimes and so should you. In fact, don't be surprised when I do." Some aren't even ashamed by it. Ever been shocked by a social media post from someone who claims Christ and think, "Wow, they probably shouldn't be doing that." Grace can give permission to sin instead of prohibiting sin.

I CAN'T STOP IT! GRACE GRANTS THE GREEN LIGHT!

HAVE YOU EVER RUN A red light thinking that it was still green? I know I have. We do the same with grace. We use it as a green light to live our own way. Consider the common little phrase "I'm under grace." I've heard this one repeatedly. I've heard people in the midst of sinful living say, "Well, God doesn't seem to care. It's all good because I'm under grace. I mean he's already paid for it, right? My standing with God can't be affected, so I can go do whatever I want." Instead of grace acting as the stop sign, or better yet, the guardrail to stop our sin, we use it as a green light to continue in sin. I have had someone say to me before, "Dave, you don't understand the struggle I face. I don't know how to stop." While I wish it were true, grace doesn't grant us approval to live whatever way we want. You know what happens when you get into sin and just can't stop? It just keeps entangling you and eventually, you ask…how do I get out?

NO ONE WILL FIND OUT! GRACE GIVES COVER!

HAVE YOU EVER BEEN CAUGHT red-handed doing something you shouldn't have been doing? I remember doing this quite often as a child. It's one thing to confess that we "just can't help it," but it's another level when we follow it up with "Well, at least no one's going to find out." It's one thing to use grace as an excuse, but to use it as a top-secret cover-up takes it to an entirely different level. The grace of God becomes a lockbox to hold all of our secrets. "Listen, if I just do this, no one's going to find out. It's not hurting anybody. I'll take it to the grave with me." And without knowing it, the excuse of grace actually poisons us instead of releasing us.

Here's the point. If we don't understand what grace is or does, we will naturally make grace a napkin that wipes our mess away instead of the motivation to surrender. Slowly, grace becomes an idol. It gets manipulated and twisted to use it for what "I" want. This is not only a faulty view of grace but also a faulty view of the gospel. That's why Paul emphatically says in Romans 6:2, "By no means!" In the Greek it's the emphatic words *Mē genomai*, which comes from the root word "to be." Literally, Paul is yelling, *"It can't be!"* No way…no how! He says, "This is not the gospel." See, the gospel isn't merely the question of whether you will go to heaven when you die. Yes, it's certainly an important part of the gospel, but not the gospel in its entirety. If that's what you believe the gospel is—if I die tonight, I get to go to heaven—then you're missing a big portion of what the gospel does in your life.

This thinking sees grace only as a get-out-of-hell-free card. That's certainly not the full biblical picture of grace. Grace is not just the idea that God makes an agreement to wipe away our sin, only to allow us to keep on sinning. As if we have been given a divine VISA card with an unlimited balance of the blood of Jesus to be applied whenever we want. Paul says, "By no means." Grace doesn't mean we get to do whatever we want…and it's not just if you were to die today, you will see Jesus…it's if you wake up tomorrow, will you live for Jesus? If you wake up tomorrow, what will your life mean? What will be your focus? Grace grants us the power to live this new life in Jesus. Paul is making the argument that more sin doesn't mean more grace. More grace actually means less sin. If you get what grace gives, you actually get less sin. It doesn't permit unrighteousness, it brings righteousness. It radically changes your heart from the inside out.

GRACE'S INVITATION

Now, LET ME MAKE AN extremely important point. Grace doesn't mean we all of a sudden stop sinning; it doesn't mean we stop struggling. Let's be honest—the struggle is real sometimes. Sometimes my faith feels like a paper cup floating in the ocean during a hurricane. Some days I feel like victory is easy, but other days it seems like a slow struggle just to overcome. What grace means is that we never stop striving. We keep going after it. It alters our life. It alters our understanding. It brings a clearer perspective of our own pleasures and habits, and changes our views about them. It says, "I want to live for something more."

Now the obvious question is, how does this happen? You guessed it; Romans 6 answers this in verses 3 and 4. "Do you not know that all of us who have been baptized into Christ Jesus were baptized into his death? We were buried therefore with him by baptism into death, in order that, just as Christ was raised from the dead by the glory of the Father, we too might walk in newness of life." Paul gives us the proof that we don't have to continue in sin. Grace doesn't have to be an idol for my desires…instead, it can bring me exactly what Christ has already conquered on my behalf. Grace affords us an escape and invites us to surrender. So the question is, how does grace do it?

Know—He says first of all it starts with knowledge. We must know the work of grace. In Romans 6:3, Paul says you've been baptized with Jesus in his death and raised with him in his resurrection. This reminds me of a summer I took my two younger boys to a local community pool for a day together. This community park has multiple pools and some pretty nice water slides. So after some time swimming, my boys wanted to venture to the bigger diving board area. I decided to take a little rest and watch them. Of course, everything is a competition, so I agreed to give them skill points on their dives.

As my kids were having fun, I couldn't help but notice a curious interaction between a fellow dad and his child. He was encouraging his son to swim in the deep end of the pool. I thought nothing of it because that is one of the unwritten roles of dads...challenging our kids to test their limits. The problem came when the little boy, probably five or six at the time, was struggling to stay afloat. You could tell that he was having trouble swimming, so much so that he started drowning. The lifeguard in me sat up, and the dad in me was greatly concerned. But oddly, the child's dad stood at the edge of the pool watching his son struggle to stay afloat and clearly wasn't going to do anything about it. Eventually the dad yelled out to his son, "Hey buddy, just hang in there. You'll be fine. Just hang on. You'll be okay." Now, I have to confess. I wanted to yell as loud as I could, "That's the problem...he has nothing to hang on to! He's in the middle of the deep end and he's nearly drowning." It blew my mind that his dad was just lackadaisically calling out for him to hang on.

Think about this for a moment. This is exactly the opposite of what God does for us through grace. Romans 6 says, "Know the work of grace. Just as Christ was crucified and buried, and then he was raised to life...you can bank your life on his work through grace." Why? Because just as Christ died and was buried and rose again, you were once dead, blind, and totally unable, but you've been brought back to life. You've received newness of life. It is *he* who brought us from ashes to beauty. It is *he* who pulled us out of the dirt. It is *he* who pulls us from the slime of sin. We can hang on to this truth because we *know* this is the work of grace. It's not just a "hang on" mentality. It's hold on to the one thing that you know will keep you afloat when you might be going under.

Count—Credit what grace offers you. If you continue reading in Romans 6, Paul describes how grace is used by Christ to undo our sin. The summary statement is found in verse 11, "So you also must consider yourselves dead to sin and alive to God in Christ Jesus." Notice the word *consider*, or *reckon* in some translations. The word *consider* is the Greek word *logizomai*, which literally means "to count." But it's more than just counting one, two, three, four, five; it's a banking or accounting term that means to credit money to a particular account. In the context, it means to count one thing as if it were another.

I would compare this to the wild card in a card game. It can be used to replace or account for any other card in the deck. That's the picture. He says, "Now reckon yourselves dead to sin and alive to God." Count on it. It's the wild card. If grace has indeed done its work in your life, count the benefits that it brings. Grace has carried newness to you. Christ has given us a new story. This means that there is not only acceptance in Jesus but also responsibility from Jesus. Grace credits our account and then makes our lives count for something far more…and Christ is the one who moves us toward it.

Apply—Apply the power of grace. Money can't just sit in an account. It's got to be applied. It has to be spent. Notice what Paul says in Romans 6:12–14,

> *Let not sin therefore reign in your mortal body, to make you obey its passions. Do not present your members to sin as instruments for unrighteousness, but present yourselves to God as those who have been brought from death to life, and your members to God as instruments for righteousness. For sin will have no dominion over you, since you are not under law but under grace.*

You see what he's saying? "What are you going to serve? Are you going to serve sin, which only leads to more condemnation and ultimately to death and dying things? Or will you serve Christ because you have been motivated by grace? How will your life be applied? Will grace abound to sin, or will grace abound to righteousness?" This passage surges in verse 14, "Sin has no more dominion over us." Sin doesn't have to win. Grace has won. It's waking up every day and saying, "Sin, you don't live here anymore!" I don't have to give way to you. I can overcome by the power of Christ. As I apply grace, sin doesn't have room for victory. We live so overwhelmed in the victory of Christ that sin is squeezed from its ability in our life. God's grace doesn't lead us to an excuse for sin, but an invitation to surrender. As we know, count, and apply the work of Christ at every moment, we accept that invitation.

Is grace an idol that frees you to sin, or is grace the means by which you serve Christ? Is grace merely a napkin to wipe away the mess of sin, or is it the napkin that leads us to serve at the beckoning of our Master, Jesus Christ? If sin abounds, it's grace-based idolatry. Of course, at times it will be visible, but at other times it will be invisible. If grace abounds, it leads to a greater Master and ultimately to a life of righteousness.

Now there are three questions I want to end this chapter with. These questions will help you know whether you are living grace in its intended form or if you have made it an idol:

1. WHERE IS SIN REIGNING IN YOUR LIFE TODAY?

Is it reigning in relationships? If you are enslaved to relationships, you'll begin to find disappointment in them. Eventually, you will manipulate relationships for your own gain or you will be greatly disappointed and dissatisfied by the relationships in your life. Eventually, what was meant to bring you companionship will actually lead you to loneliness, and ultimately relational emptiness will define you.

Is it money? If you are enslaved to money, you will certainly be able to get some things you want. But those things won't satisfy you. In fact, your eyes will never be satisfied. Eventually, jealousy will burn within you because there will always be more to have.

Is it approval? If you are enslaved to approval, your life will be plagued by constant self-pity, envy, and hurt feelings. Most likely, people will always have to walk on eggshells around you. And then, slowly, inadequacy will set in.

Are you enslaved to comfort? If you are enslaved to comfort, it will lead you to pursue pleasures of food, pleasures of sexuality, or pleasures of addiction. Of course, these things will only lead to more emptiness, less fulfillment, and discomfort in your spiritual life.

Is it power? If you are enslaved to power, you will slowly become domineering, vengeful, and, potentially, harsh and even abusive. Least of all, you will most likely start talking about yourself most of the time.

2. IS YOUR UNDERSTANDING OF GRACE CAUSING YOU TO RESIST SIN OR RESIST SURRENDER?

If I get grace and I don't have to give in to sin, am I resisting sin or am I resisting surrender to Christ? Every temptation is a directional moment. It beckons one of these directions. In which direction is grace leading me?

3. IS GRACE CAUSING YOU TO BE SERIOUS ABOUT GOD'S COMMANDS WITHOUT FALLING INTO DESPAIR?

Let me explain what I mean by this. When you consider what Paul wrote in Romans chapters 5 and 6, do you say, "Man, another command, another expectation, another thing that God wants from me"? Does it leave you in despair? If you make grace an idol, and manipulate grace toward your desires, it will lead you into misery? It will lead you into bondage, corruption, slavery, and eventually you will view the commands of God as a form of despair. Grace should reveal how beautiful and urgent the commands of Jesus are. It doesn't demand our perfection, but it does motivate our striving. A striving that pursues Christlikeness brings freedom from the "anything goes" mentality many have adopted in their Christian journeys. Instead, it can lead us to a satisfying freedom found in serving Christ. It's an exponentially better way to live.

When my boys were much younger, we had this amazing trampoline in our backyard. We would jump at every chance we could. Each time the boys and I would get on the trampoline, they would begin yelling, "Blaster! Blaster! Blaster!" Blaster was a game that the boys and I made up. I would have them sit in the middle of the trampoline and I would double-jump blast them as high as I could. A few of my boys were a little less fearful than others. So they would scream, "Higher! Higher! Higher!" Of course, as long as Mom wasn't looking, I would bounce them as hard and as high as I could.

One specific moment will be trapped in my memory forever. I blasted my son Caleb into the air and I could tell almost immediately that I had blasted him a little too much. He wasn't only going higher but also going forward. Without a doubt, he was flying off the trampoline toward our concrete patio. Disaster was certainly waiting in the wings. My immediate thought was, "My wife is going to kill me!" There is not an excuse good enough on earth for this one. My second thought was concerning what kind of pain my son is going to experience. As he flew through the air, there was an absolutely helpless feeling. There was nothing I could do now. I watched in slow motion as my son flew out of the trampoline and hit…the big safety net that surrounded the trampoline. Thank goodness that we purchased the net package. Back in my day, we didn't have safety nets. But thankfully, my son received the benefit of the surrounding net that brought him safely bouncing back into the jump area. As I looked at him, I could see the fear in his eyes as he was thinking, "What could have just happened?" It was only made worse by the fear he saw in my eyes. It easily could have been the end of his life.

Can I tell you…that's grace. Grace is the safety net that keeps us in the sweet spot of surrender. We don't have to fly off into sin. We can stay in the center of God's grace…God's righteousness. Yes, I might struggle. I might even fall a couple of times. But grace is the net that not only keeps us where we need to be but also catches us when we fall.

NOW WHAT?

Read: Romans 3-6; Ephesians 2:1-3

Discuss:

1. Describe depravity: How does Romans 5 describe how our fallen nature is transferred to us? In what ways do you struggle with this doctrine?

2. Describe the difference between our fallen state of sin and what Christ offers through grace (Romans 5:15-21): How has grace abounded more than our sin?

3. Paul moves to an interesting question at the beginning of Romans 6. How does grace become an idol that causes us to excuse our sin instead of strive against our sin? In what ways do you see grace used as a napkin to wipe our messes (sin) away instead of a motivation for godly living (give some examples of how we do this both pridefully and passively)?

4. According to Romans 6, how should the grace of God be applied to our lives? How does Christ's death and resurrection motivate righteousness? How does grace act as the great motivator?

5. In what areas of your life has grace become an excuse for sinfulness?

Pray:

Pray that God's grace would be the vehicle to move you away from sin and into righteousness

Memorize/Meditate:

"What shall we say then? Are we to continue in sin that grace may abound? By no means! How can we who died to sin still live in it? Do you not know that all of us who have been baptized into Christ Jesus were baptized into his death? We were buried therefore with him by baptism into death, in order that, just as Christ was raised from the dead by the glory of the Father, we too might walk in newness of life" (Romans 6:1-4).

CHAPTER FOUR

INSECURE GRACE

...to the praise of his glorious grace, with which he has blessed us in the Beloved. (Ephesians 1:6)

U NDOUBTEDLY, IF WE ARE TO fully appreciate the impact of grace in our lives, we have to understand the influence grace has on our identity. Identity is at the core of grace's work in our lives. Oddly enough, the word *identity* could be considered a buzzword in our culture today. There are tons of books written on the topic of *identity* and even more written on *Christian identity*. There is a deep search for answers to questions like "What is our identity?" Or even more precisely, "Who are you?" and "Where are you going?"

Whenever I hear the word *identity*, I can't help but think of "Senior Superlatives." Now, I don't know if your high school did this, but my high school allowed students to present "Superlatives" at the end of their senior year. Basically, the idea was that you could vote on these pithy prophetic statements that you think would most likely come true in each student. Seniors would be named things like "most likely to become president," "most likely to get married," "most likely to have kids first," "most likely to get a college degree," "most likely to be a future dancer," and so on and so forth. In essence, these were funny awards given to fellow students based upon their character and what you thought the person would accomplish in their lives.

In my senior year, I was actually given two—one built upon who I was and another as a sort of joke. No doubt ironic, one of them declared that I was the most likely to become a pastor. I went to a Christian high school and helped lead a Bible study throughout my time there. I was even a student speaker in chapel on a few occasions, so that superlative came as no surprise. Of course, it was also an extremely gracious compliment. However, the second was an interesting contrast. Now remember, one was supposed to be a bit humorous… but it was also disheartening. So my classmates declared I was the most likely "to get in trouble with the law."

I have no clue how my classmates correlated these two immensely different ideas. I mean, please believe me, I never did anything illegal in high school. I was a pretty good student. But I have to confess, I did have a bit of an edge about me. Of all the students in my class, I did grow up in what some would consider the inner-city area of my hometown. Specifically, in a neighborhood between two large areas that were considered lower income project housing.[1] There was also a joke that went around that said, "Dave kind of likes to live on the edge…a crazy side." Of course, never anything illegal, but certainly edgy, willing to try anything that would be fun. A daredevil if you will.[2] Thankfully, my classmates were false prophets, and this superlative has never come true. Although, I'm still watching my back on this one and praying it never does in the future.

The superlatives were certainly funny, but they were predominantly meant to be small statements that give subtle insights into your identity. Innocent fun, but also somewhat true. Who are you? How would you describe yourself? How do you see yourself? These are the greatest questions you can ever ask yourself. Whatever your answer might be to these questions, they will give you keen insights and key indicators of how you view your identity. It is the truest thing that you think about yourself. How you view yourself not only will define your identity, but it can also be life altering and eternity shaping.

The journey toward our identity starts at the beginning of life. We start building identity at a pretty young age, don't we? Take babies for example. We say things like, "Well, they're the cute one of the bunch," or "they're the not-so-cute one of the bunch," or "they're the chubby one" or "the skinny one," or "they're the smart one" or "the funny one." And while life changes, this identity-building language

---

1   I absolutely loved my childhood in this area. Proud to be a "West-Ender" in Hagerstown, MD.

2   Ironically, I'm not even the craziest on my church staff. If you know our church, I will let your imagination run wild on this one.

doesn't. We eventually become school-aged students and begin to describe children in a similar way. Some are the athletic ones, the creative ones, the artistic ones, the geeks, and the jocks.

As these identities grow, slowly nicknames begin to be built around these names…some of them negative, some of them positive, all with the potential of defining who you are and who you might become. And then you know what happens? We hit middle school. And we face a season of extreme confusion. We have no clue who we are. We get called all kinds of different names and get encouraged to try all of these different things. We are told, "You ought to try this, you ought to attempt that, and you ought to be like this." No wonder there's mass confusion at this age.

Of course, these transitional years lead to the wonderful years we call high school. This is a time where you are not only trying to figure out who you are but also trying to figure out what you're supposed to do. From friend groups to interests, from the desperate need of guidance to the fight for independence, we are frantically searching for something that will settle our search for identity. Eventually, we get to college where all of the lessons we have learned drive us to decisions that will define the rest of our lives. What job will we have? Who will we marry? How many kids will we have? And even after all of these things, we still attempt to find and define our identity. Identity could be considered the journey of life…the Holy Grail of living. And our search would prove that identity does determine everything.

Take a moment to think about your identity. How would you answer this question:

If we're being entirely honest, we might answer this question with some description that we believe is true about us. We might say: I am young. I am old. I am rich. I am poor. I'm smart. I'm dumb. I'm loved. I'm hated. I'm single. I'm married. I'm divorced. I'm desperate. I'm successful. I'm a failure. Others might answer the statement with what they do: I am a doctor; mechanic; teacher; stay-at-home parent; pastor; lawyer or other similar answer.

What would you put in that blank? Identity determines everything. It determines the direction of your life and how you will respond in certain situations. It will reveal itself in relationships. And it can alter the trajectory of your life. And you want to know something particularly fascinating? Our pursuit of personal identity can actually cause us to take grace and misalign it. Our hunt for identity could actually be leading us to a mistaken and misapplied view of grace, and we might not even realize it. Eventually, we find ourselves in a deeper identity crisis, a spiritual identity crisis.

IDENTITY CRISIS

OVER AND OVER AGAIN, THE Scriptures speak to our identity. We don't always see it at first glance, but it's embedded throughout. There are many passages I could mention that reveal where we can find true identity, but probably none more than the book of Ephesians. It is a letter written with spiritual identity in mind. Now if you look at most commentaries or resources on the book of Ephesians, most will describe it as a book with two distinct divisions. Specifically, Paul spends the first three chapters describing doctrinal truths and then the last three chapters focusing on how to live…things like marriage, kids, forgiveness, conflict management, workplace relationships, spiritual warfare, and a host of other life issues. This is no doubt true. But that's only partly correct. This thought treats Ephesians primarily as a book of doctrine or a practical guide for living. But there's something deeper that God is telling us through this book. It's not found in a simple reading of the book, but it becomes abundantly evident when you understand a bit of the history of the book, specifically regarding life in the city of Ephesus, the namesake of the book. You could say, life in the city of Ephesus was all about identity.

IDENTITY OF ACCOMPLISHMENT

EPHESUS WAS ONE OF THE most impressive and intimidating cities of the ancient world. It was on a seaport right at the intersection of what is today Europe and Asia, which made it one of the main trade-hubs of the Roman Empire. It was both cosmopolitan and multicultural. It boasted one of the largest libraries in history, and many of the world's most prestigious scholars lived there. This most likely produced a well-educated society. There is no doubt that if you had walked through the city of Ephesus in the first century, you would sense a feeling of tremendous accomplishments. This led to immense national pride in the heart of each Ephesian.

IDENTITY OF EFFORTS

RELIGIOUSLY, IT WAS A SMORGASBORD. Religious fervor was at the core of the Ephesian life. The city housed fifty different types of temples. Imagine that…fifty temples. But one of them stood out as the gem among all the others. It was the largest temple of the ancient world, dedicated to Artemis[3] (considered the twin sister of Apollo), a Greco-Roman goddess of hunting, wild animals, sexuality, childbirth, and virginity. Today, it's considered one of the Seven Wonders of the Ancient World. As a result of so many temples and religious options, people dedicated time and wealth to religious worship. You could imagine much of the city was immeasurably engrossed in their religious duties and personal efforts. Everyday, you would be reminded to do more, serve more, sacrifice more, and give more.

IDENTITY OF SIN

SEXUAL IMMORALITY WAS A BOOMING industry in Ephesus. Most of the temples offered some kind of prostitution as part of the worship rituals. Sex was a form of worship, specifically as it was dedicated to the gods of sexuality. There was probably a sign outside the city that said,

---

3   Diana is actually the Roman equivalent of this Greek goddess. The Romans adopted many of the Greek gods and goddesses and renamed them.

"What happens in Ephesus stays in Ephesus!" This created a culture of sexual perversion and confusion. You could only imagine the sexual baggage that most people carried in Ephesus.

There can be no doubt that these religious, social, economic, and educational experiences helped shape the identity of the Ephesians. But can you imagine what happened when Christianity came to the city of Ephesus? This would not have been considered a Christian-friendly place. Person after person had sinful pasts. There were deep skeletons in their closets. They certainly had grave regrets that became deeply connected to their identities. As people came to Christ, you could hear the barrage of questions like, "How do I live out this newfound Christian faith in this culture?" and "What does identity in Christ look like after all that I've done?"

And this is the crowd, now redeemed, to whom Paul writes this letter. Can you say "identity crisis"? They had their identity as Ephesians and now their new identity in Christ. You can imagine it created an internal conflict for many of them, if not all of them. If identity determines behavior, what does it look like to live as a follower of Christ in that type of context? What does it look like to stand in grace? Paul writes the book of Ephesians to deal with these questions. We could argue whether our culture is similar or not, but we do know these are the same questions that you and I ask today. How can we stand in grace? How do we live our Christian identity in a culture bombarded with identity thieves?

IDENTITY DEFINED

PAUL STARTS HIS LETTER TO the Ephesians with a passage that speaks deeply to identity. A simple reading of chapter 1 would leave you thinking that Paul is merely rambling on and on. If you think this, you aren't wrong. Verses 3 through 14 are actually one complete sentence in the Greek.[4] It's a sentence that theologians love but English teachers hate. It's one long, Spirit-inspired, run-on sentence. And it's incredibly intentional. These verses show that God's plan is complete. That there is no missing link in his plan for us and, consequently, there is nothing missing in the formation of our identities. We're going to look at just a few of these truths, but if you could paint a picture of this passage, it would be a beautiful portrait of the Trinity. It starts with what the Father has done in the past, followed by how the Son redeems us in the present, and finally how the Spirit prepares us for the future.

But all of this finds its origins in the beginning of the passage with a beautiful praise to God (1:3). The word *blessing* is the Greek word εὐλογητός, *eulogétos*, which is where we get our word *eulogy*. If you've ever been to a funeral or wedding, the eulogy is the name given for the message. It is a blessing given to a person who has passed or the couple being wed. Paul declares that everything that comes after is meant to cause us to praise God. Why? Because he has blessed us with every spiritual blessing in the heavenly places (1:3). God is blessed, because he has blessed us so abundantly.[5] I love what one pastor recommended as the translation of this verse. "Blessed be the blessed Blesser, who has blessed us with blessed blessings." That is literally what it's saying. It's poetic. But more importantly, notice that these blessings are not just merely physical blessings. These blessings are spiritual in nature. Notice their location "in the heavenlies." This phrase is only found here in the Scriptures. Paul is emphasizing that we are blessed, not merely physically, not merely emotionally, not even mentally...we are blessed spiritually. And our spiritual blessings are found in the arena of grace, a place where we can find lasting identity. Every believer possesses this overwhelming, blessed grace.

So we have been given all of these spiritual blessings found in the arena of grace. But how do these blessings relate to our identities?

---

4   It's actually 202 words that make up this one sentence.
5   An interesting note: The word *blessed* is in the aorist Greek tense. Meaning that it is something that happened in the past moment but has continuing results. This means that what God has done in the past for us continues to bless us over and over again.

This passage gives plenty of answers, but I want to highlight two of them that are explicitly connected to our identity:

_____

GOD CHOSE US BY HIS GRACE

> *...even as he chose us in him before the foundation of the world, that we should be holy and blameless before him.* (Ephesians 1:4)

GOD CHOSE US BY GRACE. God chose you, believer, by his grace. The word *chose* in verse 4 is a fascinating word. It's the Greek word ἐκλέγω, *eklego*. When I was taking Greek in seminary, I memorized this word by using the wordplay "L'eggo my Eggo." You may have seen those Eggo Waffle commercials that show the difficulty of keeping your fingers off someone else's waffle. That's this word. It's actually a compound word, *ek*, which means "out of" and *lego*, which means "to choose." Put them together and you literally have the idea *to choose out of*.

Now, I know what just happened in a lot of our minds. You may have gotten a little nervous. "Oh, Dave, did you just say that we are chosen?" It seems in Christian circles the theological idea of being chosen scares a lot of people, even though we see it throughout the Scripture generally and here in Ephesians specifically. God chose us. But that's not actually the scary part. It says in verse 4 that "he chose us in him before the foundation of the world."

Now before we go any further, I want to confess that some things in Scripture that are mentioned as matters of fact are difficult for us to grasp. They are true but hard to understand fully. If we are being honest, most of us have no problem saying that God is in control, God is sovereign, but how that plays out in our lives leaves us with great questions. Most of us aren't going to argue against the Scriptures proclaiming that God does and can do whatever he desires.

Actually, I would go so far as to also say we don't have an issue with the fact that God chooses? For example, we know that God chose nationally. God chose the people of Israel as a nation for his promises and blessings. We have no problem believing that, do we? We also don't have any problem with saying that God chooses vocationally. God chose Samson as a judge, David as a king, Jeremiah as a prophet, Esther as a queen, and even Jesus is called the Chief Cornerstone chosen by the Father.

We have no problem saying that God chooses. Questions arise when we consider the extent of God's choosing as it relates to our salvation, whether we are the ones chosen or not. Because in our minds, we equate choosing to being selected for a kickball game in elementary school...you better not be last or left out. When it comes to spiritual election, the answer has much bigger implications and we know it. You know what is most interesting? In Ephesians, Paul doesn't speak or act as if God's sovereignty in salvation is any big deal. He states it as a matter of fact and he moves on. It's as if the readers would just respond with "Well duh...of course!" He simply says, "God chose you in him before the foundation of the world."

When we talk about spiritual, sovereign election, there are two predominant views...passive and active. The difference boils down to this...who has the ultimate choice in salvation, God or man? The passive view says that God chose me because I believed in him and he knew it beforehand. In essence, it is saying that we cooperated with God and chose him and therefore he chose us. So there's a bit of work on our part. The active view says, "I believed because God chose me."[6] It's the idea that there is one activity, and it is the activity of God, and he has accomplished it all. That his choosing is not precipitated upon anything we've done, it's not a reward for us, it is that God has done it because we can't. It's solely based upon his grace. In the first view (passive), man has some role. In the second view (active), there is only one who is active, and it's God.

Now if we go back to the beginning of our study, our definition of grace seems to demand the active view. Remember, grace is undeserved and unmerited. This is the doctrine of depravity...our total and utter inability. This means that if God does not elect, no one can or will

---

6   In theological circles another name for the active view is the
     monergistic view.

be saved. In the theological world, this is called the doctrine of sovereign grace. Let me give you a more proper definition:

> ### Sovereign Grace
> **Based upon the total inability of man to initiate salvation, God, by an act of grace, sovereignly chose from eternity those who would be saved from sin's bondage, through the effective work of Christ's death and resurrection, by initiating their repentance and faith in Christ.**

This doctrine connects God's sovereignty with his grace. Simply put, God knew and God acted. God took the first step, because we couldn't. He chose us because we would always choose wrongly. By the way, do you know or remember the story of John Newton? He was the captain of a slave trade boat that he gave up only to later became a pastor. He wrote a song called "Faith's Review and Expectation." Have you ever heard of it? Most likely not by that title. We know it from the first phrase of the song, "Amazing Grace." The whole song is about the story of faith's origination and expectation. There is a beautiful lyric in the song that says, "'Twas grace that taught my heart to fear." You know what Newton was describing? The active view of grace. It was God who brought grace to us and grace only that allowed my heart to learn what it needed to learn.

Now you might ask an obvious and appropriate question: "What about free will?" Does this mean that we are simply robots without free will? The answer is absolutely "No!" We certainly have free will. That's the argument of the Scripture. We have free will, but what do we do with our free will? We saw the work of free will in the last chapter. When given over to our own free will, we consistently choose wrongly, sinfully…we choose idols. Our choice goes bad. So what does God do? God works in the hearts of those he has chosen; and as a result we freely believe Christ because we want to believe Christ. God doesn't bypass our wills; he overcomes our blindness and grants us the faith to believe. And so, God chose us and in response we choose him freely. In other words, despite the tension between God's sovereignty and our free will, the Bible teaches both. They are complementary. God awakens us, we choose him as a result. God chooses and whosoever will. That's the biblical picture.

These truths remind me of a men's event that my church was sponsoring. I was asked to speak at a men's Eat and Skeet Shooting event. Now let's be honest, you can't get any better than that. Eat a big breakfast and shoot some big guns. Manhood at its finest. Well, after breakfast and my message, we all went out to shoot clays. They divided the men into groups of four to five to shoot at different stations at the gun club. Uniquely, every station offered a different perspective of the clays and thus a different angle of shots. Some went in the air, others went along the ground…some came toward you and others away.

There was one specific station where the clay disk would fly across the ground, and I noticed one person in our group who would wait until the clay hit the ground, and then he would shoot. All five of his shots were exactly the same. The clay hit the ground, and then his shot would ring out. Ironically, after each shot he would cheer as if he was a master marksman. Now if I could be honest, I wish I had thought of this idea. I mean how brilliant was that! My score would have certainly been a lot better. Funny thing, all the other guys in my group knew what had just happened. But we never said a word. Why ruin this guy's fun?

That's exactly how it is when we attempt to figure out the apparent contradiction of free will vs. God's sovereign choice. It's as if we're letting the clay hit the ground and saying, "I've got this figured out; I'm a marksman." As one friend always says, "It's like throwing a dart and then drawing a circle around it." It is God who has chosen us by an act of grace. Our job is to accept the mystery.

Back to Ephesians…Paul explains three main ways that God chooses us:

GOD CHOOSES INTENTIONALLY

GOD CHOOSES US INTENTIONALLY. IT says in verse 4, "Even as he chose us in him." We see this throughout biblical history. Abraham was an old man when God revealed, "I've chosen you. I'm going to give you a child and I'm going to make a nation of you." There was the small boy, Samuel, who heard from God while serving in the House of the Lord… and God called him into the priesthood. There was a small shepherd boy named David, and God calls him to be the king. God makes these choices intentionally. God said to the prophet Isaiah,

> For I am God, and there is no other; I am God, and there is none like me, declaring the end from the beginning and from ancient times things not yet done, saying, "My counsel shall stand, and I will accomplish all my purpose." (Isaiah 46:9–10)

Paul wrote to the Romans, "I will have mercy on whom I have mercy, and I will have compassion on whom I have compassion" (Romans 9:15). God's choices are always intentional because they are always according to his perfect plan.

GOD CHOOSES ETERNALLY

GOD CHOOSES US ETERNALLY. NOTICE Ephesians 1:4 continues, "Even as he chose us in him before the foundation of the world." People were in the heart of God before history was written. God's hand wasn't forced, he wasn't responding to a crisis, he wasn't ratifying human choices, he wasn't choosing on the basis of us. It says, "Before the foundation of the world…" He was confident in his choosing. In fact, he chose sovereignly based upon his own character, his own identity. He is the only source and reasoning behind the choosing, not us. I love how Charles Spurgeon describes this: "I am so glad that God chose me before the foundation of the world because He never would have chosen me after I was born." Isn't that so true? He already had this planned and you and I were part of that plan, regardless of what we were or have done.

GOD CHOOSES PURPOSEFULLY

GOD CHOOSES US PURPOSEFULLY. VERSE 4 continues, "Even as he chose us in him before the foundation of the world, that we should be holy and blameless before him." Notice there's an intended direction for our choosing. If you're a follower of Christ, it's not enough that you've been chosen for salvation, but you've been chosen to be holy and blameless. This means that the God who started and initiated the work, who planned it before the beginning of the world, will one day present us holy and blameless. That is the beautiful work of God's goodness and grace. Our new identity is tied to the fact that he chose us by his grace. Our identity is wrapped in God's choice of us.

GOD ADOPTED US BY HIS GRACE

THE SECOND OBSERVATION FROM EPHESIANS 1 that relates to our identity is that God adopted us by his grace. "In love, he predestined us for adoption as sons through Jesus Christ according to the purpose of his will" (v. 5). God has predestined us to adoption. The Greek word προορίζω, *proorizó*, translated "predestination," has been the center of much debate throughout the years. There are entire books written on this topic alone. I in no way want to downplay all the scholarly effort toward this concept. But I think the simplest explanation is sometimes the best.

I especially find it interesting that Paul doesn't spend any effort attempting to explain the concept. It's expected that the Ephesians, and consequently we, would understand what he means by it. The word *predestined* is a compound word, *pre-destined*, which means "to pre-determine or decide beforehand." Now some might ask, "Well, doesn't that mean he knows what we're going to do?" Simply put, no! It means that God is deciding for himself beforehand what he is going to do. God determines everything with the end in view because for God, time has already been accomplished. It's already done in His eyes, because he is timeless.

I have to confess, it gives me a headache just thinking about it. Remember the term "Blessed despair!" This is one of those moments. It reminds me of when you are making preparations for a vacation. If you're seeking out a travel agent to prepare for your vacation, you better have at least a rough idea as to where you would like to go. It would be like going to a travel agent and saying, "I'd like to plan a trip." They respond, "Where do you want to go?" And you answer, "I don't know."

Of course, they can make helpful suggestions, but at some point you have to know where you would like to go. If destination determines direction, God knows where he is taking us. This is predestination. He knows the destination. But what's even more astounding is not only that he knows what he's doing but actually where he is going to do it. Notice it wonderfully describes the direction of his choosing…our adoption. He knew beforehand that he was going to adopt us. What a beautifully magnificent concept.

Today, our view of adoption is usually focused on the need of children who find themselves in desperate situations. There are children who have lost their parents either by death or circumstances beyond their control, leaving them desperate for a permanent, stable family. However, in the first century, it was based not upon the need of children but on the legacy of an heir. A much different perspective than ours today, but a needed reality nonetheless.

People without biological children in the first century would look at their estate and say, "You know what, I need somebody to pass this on to." And so they would adopt someone so that their legacy would be assured. That person would receive a new father, a new mother, a new future, a new life form, and a new lifestyle, all wrapped in their new identity as part of a new family.

Don't miss the depth of this truth. God is telling us in Ephesians, "Not only have I chosen you, but I have chosen you in order to adopt you into my family, my legacy. To bring you into what you could never have on your own." I love what J. I. Packer said, "Adoption is the highest privilege the gospel offers."[7] Arguably, adoption could be considered higher than salvation itself. Why? Because adoption involves an intimate relationship with God, the Father.[8] Adoption is the essence of the gospel. God doesn't just save us, he takes us into his family as children and heirs. He gives us a new reality…a new identity. We've been predestined to be adopted.

---

7   J. I. Packer and Carolyn Nystrom, *Knowing God Devotional Journal: A One-Year Guide* (Downers Grove, IL: InterVarsity Press, 2009), 231.

8   Ibid.

These truths leave me both grateful and intrigued. Why in the world would God do this for us? Why? A simple yet necessary question. Well, Paul doesn't leave us void of the answer. Ephesians 1:6 answers, "To the praise of his glorious grace with which he has blessed us in the Beloved."[9] Why does God choose us and adopt us? Notice it says "to the praise of his grace." All of the work of God is meant to demonstrate the beauty of God's grace. To show us the depth of his grace, which in return leads us to praise him. If we put this all together: Election says I matter…adoption says I belong…and grace says I am accepted…all these truths shout praise to God. I matter, I belong, I'm adopted, I'm chosen, and that is our identity in Christ.

If we stop there, no doubt this is an amazing, mind-blowing, and life-altering truth. In Christ we've been chosen, in Christ we've been adopted, in Christ we've been given this overwhelming grace. Grace is once again God's sufficient instrument for our deliverance. But, and yes this is a big but, there is a problem; there is also a shadow side of this beautiful picture of grace. Before I explain what it is, I want you to know why. Whenever we begin to see the grandeur of God's gracious work for us, we start to struggle a bit. When I read passages like Ephesians 1, part of me says, "This can't be true!" "No way God would do this for me!" "If it's too good to be true, it is!" In fact, I would go so far as to say that you probably felt the same as you were reading this section. I know I did. Why is that? Because we've been taught from a young age that we better work hard, better do it right, and better give it our best.

Like many, I remember as a kid having an unwritten but firm rule that said I wasn't allowed to go outside until my homework was done. In fact, my mom would routinely remind me, "We get our work done before we play." Why? Because work always precedes play. Work trumps fun. Work defines life. I realize my mom probably didn't mean it in this way, but isn't that the way life happens? Round and round and round it goes, but the underlying message is always the same: ac-

---

9   Notice the word *Beloved* is capitalized. This is additional proof that this passage is focused on our Christian identity. We are given the beautiful distinction as the "Beloved."

complishment precedes acceptance, achievement precedes approval, identity is found in the effort. The more I do, the better I am. The more I accomplish, the greater my reputation. The more I work, the greater I'll be respected. And so, while we sing, "We are saved by amazing grace," we live by the sweat of our performance. And we are constantly challenging ourselves to "try harder." This isn't just a physical approach to life; it goes much deeper than this as it overflows into our spiritual lives. I just need to spiritually try harder. Got to show more spiritual effort. And herein lies how grace becomes an idol:

> **Grace becomes an idol when our identity is centered on our sufficiency and not set in God's sovereignty.**

Let me repeat this. Grace becomes an idol when our identity is centered on our sufficiency and not set in God's sovereignty. There can be little argument that just like the Ephesians 2,000 years ago, we are in an identity crisis. We have a deep spiritual crisis in our society today. How do I know that? Did you know that 73% of Americans claim to be Christians?[10] Obviously, the term *Christian* is a loose term in our culture. We know that can mean a lot of different things. But of the 73% claiming to be Christian, only 31% would consider themselves "practicing Christians."[11]

IDENTITY CONFUSION

If our identity determines our behavior, our behavior is exhibiting proof that we don't really know where our identity lies. And our identity certainly isn't set in a God who is sovereign and has given

---

10   Allison De Jong, "Protestants decline, more have no religion in a sharply shifting religious landscape (Poll)," *ABCNews/Beliefnet*, May 10, 2018, https://abcn.ws/2G0xoQ5.

11   "The State of the Church 2016," *Barna*, September 15, 2016, https://www.barna.com/research/state-church-2016/.

us his sovereign grace. In fact, the statistics reveal that only 57% of those who claim to be Christians believe that God is an all-powerful, all-knowing, and perfect creator who rules over the universe.[12] Only half actually believe that God is sovereign over all. I would suggest that many Christians have what we could call spiritual amnesia. We attend church, read the Bible, hope in and praise God, but in the end we forget who we are. We see it, hear it, and understand it, but then walk away unchanged. How could this be? The only answer is that we are living in our own sufficiency. Instead of being, we begin doing and a cycle of confusion begins. We're living through the identity of our own self-sufficiency.

Let me go back to the questions we asked at the beginning of this chapter. Deep yet profound questions that we are answering every day, whether we want to or not.

> **Who are you? What defines you?**
> **How do you define yourself?**
>
> **Complete this sentence: I am _____.**

Pause for a few minutes and consider these questions.
- Is it what you have or don't have?
- Is it what you do or don't do?
- Is it the job you possess or wish you had?
- Is it what you wear or don't wear?
- Is it that you're dating, married, divorced, single, heartbroken?
- Is it a career? A house? A car?
- Is it your past, good or bad?
- Is it your failures, your shortcomings, your fears?

---

12   Ibid.

-    Is it your dreams?

How did you answer those questions? If we're being honest, most of us work hard to present an image that would be considered the best version of who we are. We are left to define ourselves by the things we accomplish, the names we are given, the labels we wear, and the image we portray. And all of these are veiled in our self-sufficiency. Ironically, you know what happens when we attempt to live on our own self-sufficiencies? Insecurity. Our self-sufficiency makes a beeline to insecurity. Let me repeat that. Our self-sufficiency leads us into insecurity. Why? Because self-sufficiency is false security. For some that insecurity is obvious, but for many it masks itself in pride. Our self-sufficiency acts as security, but it's only false security; it's not even true! It doesn't actually satisfy our deepest desire for identity. It only leads us to deep insecurity.

Can I make an honest confession? One of the biggest struggles in my own life has been insecurity. If you have ever met me, you might question that statement. I come across confident, cool, and in control. Okay, the cool part could be argued. But genuinely, I tend to be a decisive leader, not tossed by the whims of insecurity. But external appearances are not always realities. Personally, I have battled insecurity throughout my entire life. In fact, there have been moments where insecurity has paralyzed me.

Even at the beginning of my ministry, as I journeyed through Bible college and seminary, I found myself attempting to accomplish things that would make sure that people were pleased and my identity looked good. This type of living almost led me to wave the white flag and actually quit ministry altogether. I was living a life of fear, self-sufficiency, and insecurity instead of resting in my identity on the sovereignty of God's gracious choice of me. I felt anonymous, abandoned, and afraid, and instead of an adopted son of the Most High, I felt like an orphan. You know what's even crazier? I started to believe what wasn't even true about me. I let the whispers in my head begin to define me instead of what God had already declared about me. And instead of resting in the sovereign grace of God, I had to continue to look for a more sufficient, greater grace.

I don't believe this confession is unique. Everything would point to the legitimacy that this is the way most of us view our lives. Instead of our identity being grounded in God's unconditional choice and loving adoption of us as Christians, we let so many other things begin to define us. We attempt to live life by our own self-sufficiency instead of being set in the sovereign grace of God.

I remember reading an intriguing article recently about an experiment that was directed a few decades ago. The experiment was called "The Scar Experiment." Dr. Robert Kleck, a psychologist at Dartmouth College, devised a social experiment that illustrated how body image affects how people think about themselves.[13] He took ten participants and asked Hollywood artists to make fake scars on their faces. They then sent the participants out into the public to gauge the reactions and feelings they experienced as strangers responded to their distorted looks.

Immediately before sending them out, Dr. Kleck gave them a few rules. First, they were not allowed to look in any mirrors or windows. Secondly, they were asked to come back in for a touch-up of the fake scar before they went out into the public. And this is where it got interesting: the team of artists took the scars off the faces of all the participants and replaced them with something that would be deemed beautiful. All of the participants believed that the scar was still there. Upon returning from their time in public, all ten of the participants came back and reported on their experience. And the results were telling. All of them reported that people looked at them poorly, some even reported looks of horror. They described people glaring at them, kids rejecting them, and many making private comments.

The most ironic thing about this experiment is that the scar wasn't even there. They received the reaction they expected. Or more

---

13   Sandra Blakeslee, "How You See Yourself: Potential for Big
        Problems," *New York Times*, February 7, 1991, https://www.nytimes.
        com/1991/02/07/news/how-you-see-yourself-potential-for-big-
        problems.html.

likely, they believed what they perceived about their own identities. Is it possible that our identity might be set on something that isn't even true? As someone once said, "A lie that is believed to be true will affect us as if it is true, even if it's absolutely false." We might see ourselves as unlovable, defective, and worthless. If you believe that, you will live that.

This is exactly where eating disorders, sexual sin, riveting fear, and overwhelming anxiety come from. Instead of allowing God's sovereign choice to adopt us and define our identities, we believe a lie. We twist the sovereign, gracious work of God for us and use it to battle our identities instead of defining our identities. Instead of living on grace alone, we live on grace for more. It leaves us needing more grace instead of living on the grace we have already been given from God.

IDENTITY RESTORED

This struggle doesn't come without an answer. Paul continues the discussion on identity in Ephesians 2. I realize this is a common salvation passage, but I've never seen this passage in this way before. The way Paul reminds them of the gospel is beyond powerful.

> And you were dead in the trespasses and sins in which you once walked, following the course of this world, following the prince of the power of the air, the spirit that is now at work in the sons of disobedience—among whom we all once lived in the passions of our flesh, carrying out the desires of the body and the mind, and were by nature children of wrath, like the rest of mankind. (Ephesians 2:1–3)

Ephesians 2 begins with a description of our identity before Christ. Notice it's all past tense. You were blind, you were enslaved, you were dead, you were overwhelmed, you were the sons of disobedience, you were children destined for wrath. Paul is using their past to ad-

dress the identity crisis found in many Ephesian Christians of the day
by demonstrating three predominant things:

We are not who we were. You are not who you were. For those who
battle insecurity…who would say, "I'm too far off"; "I'm not
enough"; "I'm marked by what I have done, my past failures,"
this passage declares that grace is unaffected by our degree of
sin. Grace doesn't make demands; it just gives. And from our
vantage point, it might seem to give to the wrong person, but
that's the work of grace. In the Gospels, we find Jesus giving to the
wrong people…the prostitutes, the rejects, the dirty, and the tax
collectors. The most extravagant sinners of Jesus' day received his
most compassionate welcome. Why? Because grace is recklessly
generous and uncomfortably promiscuous. True grace tells us we
are not who we were.

We are not what we do. A few verses later, Paul turns to the self-
sufficient, the ones who are going to attempt to find their identities
in their own efforts and works. And he says to them, "For by grace
you have been saved through faith. And this is not your own doing;
it is the gift of God, not a result of works, so that no one may boast"
(Ephesians 2:8). No one can say, "I can do it." Our identity is not
derived by our behavior and our abilities. Grace doesn't use gold
stars, time cards, or bank accounts. It doesn't keep score. It works
without requiring anything on our part. It refuses to be controlled
by our innate sense of fairness, reciprocity, and evenhandedness.
It defies our logic. It has nothing to do with earning, merit, or
deservedness. In fact, it's opposed to what is owed. There is a
liberating contradiction between what we deserve and what we
get, because grace is the gift of God.

We are what Jesus has done. This entire passage swells at verse 10,
"For we are his workmanship, created in Christ Jesus for good
works, which God prepared beforehand, that we should walk in
them." Lastly, we are what Jesus accomplished by grace. Or to put it
another way: We are not defined by what we've done or who we've

been. We're defined by what Jesus has done. That's what grace does. It doesn't define us by our attempt to accomplish something we can't. It doesn't define us by one who left us, but the One who invited us; not by one who overlooked us, but the One who chose us; not by one who ridiculed us, but the One who redeemed us; not by one who abandoned us, but by the One who adopted us as his own…Jesus.

Where do you find your identity? The doctrine of sovereign grace should give you security and sufficiency for your life. Insecurity is overwhelmed by the safety of grace, and self-sufficiency is overcome by the ability of grace. We do have an identity crisis in our world today. This is especially seen in the fear and insecurities of many. People are living by their past mistakes, by the labels they've been given, by the way they attempt to find their own identity. May we remember our identities are not achieved; they're received in Jesus. Don't be duped by false securities. Don't be conned by thinking that work, relationships, careers, productivity, bank accounts, and success make us who we are. That's a false idol grace. True biblical grace tells us that Jesus has established our identity. Our identity has been chosen for us through our adoption in the family of God, because grace firmly sets our identity in the plan and purpose of God.

NOW WHAT?

Read: Ephesians 1-2, Ephesians 4:1-2; John 6

Discuss:

1. How do you see the identity crisis in our world today? Why do so many Christians struggle with their spiritual identity in Christ? In what ways do our identity struggles demonstrate themselves mentally, emotionally, and physically?

2. Define sovereign election: Why is sovereign election such a difficult doctrine to understand? Describe the passive and active views of election: How can sovereign election and free will be understood as compliments instead of contradictions?

3. How should the doctrines of election and adoption confirm our spiritual identity? How does grace become an idol of self-sufficiency and insecurity? Is it true that self-sufficiency and insecurity go hand in hand? Today, what types of things do people put their sufficiency and security in?

4. How should your knowledge of God's sovereign election and adoption enhance your view of grace? How can grace settle any identity crisis you might be having? Give some real-life examples of people who live with a grace-based identity and are walking worthy of their calling in Christ.

Pray:

Ponder the beauty of God's sovereignty in your life. Pray that your identity will be settled in God's sovereignty.

Memorize/Meditate:

"Blessed be the God and Father of our Lord Jesus Christ, Who has blessed us in Christ with every spiritual blessing in the heavenly places, even as He chose us in Him before the foundation of the world, that we should be holy and blameless before Him. In love He predestined us for adoption to Himself as sons through Jesus Christ, according to the purpose of His will, to the praise of His glorious grace, with which He has blessed us in the Beloved" (Ephesians 1:3-6).

CHAPTER FIVE

Immature Grace

But grow in the grace and knowledge of our Lord and Savior Jesus Christ. (2 Peter 3:18)

I PROBABLY DON'T HAVE TO CONVINCE you that there is a progression of life. There's an unwritten but understood expectation that a baby in the womb will eventually become an infant. An infant is expected to become a toddler who crawls and walks. The toddler will become a child, and the child will become a teenager, and the teenager will eventually not want to be a kid anymore. They will want to be seen as an adult. Then, there is driving, college, a career, and eventually marriage and a family. Of course, life is funny. We end up being an adult wishing we could go back and do it all over again. Oh…the irony!

I have many memories of my own childhood, but also of the small yet reflective things I have seen in my own sons. One of the fond memories I have with my boys is when they were toddlers. When they ate in their highchairs, my wife and I would incite a funny and adorable response. We asked a simple question but expected a vibrant response. "How big are you?" They looked at us with these big eyes and huge smiles, and responded (of course we taught them this), "This big!" With outstretched arms as far as they could extend. Naturally, it ended in fanatical laughter over our exaggerated expressions. Of course, being the dad that I am, I recently went up to my teenage son and asked him this same question. He stared at me oddly, as if to say, "Dad, what's wrong with you?" I said, "No, I'm serious…how big are you? Remember you use to say, 'This big!'" And he said, "Dad, you're just plain weird!"

THE EXPECTATION FOR SPIRITUAL GROWTH

THERE IS A FOUNDATIONAL EXPECTATION in life that we're going to physically grow up, that we're going to physically progress. When physical growth doesn't happen, something has radically gone wrong. In the same way, we are expected to spiritually grow. In fact, throughout the Scripture physical development is used as a picture of our spiritual development. Salvation is called a new birth because salvation acts as the entry point into the Christian life. But it doesn't end there. It's the starting point, not the ending point. And throughout the Bible, God uses the universal metaphor of childhood and adulthood as a picture of the expected growth in Christ. Of course, physically, we know there is a desperate need for a combination of food and exercise, sustenance and activity. But what about our spiritual growth? What is it that grows us? We find throughout the Scriptures that the basis of our spiritual growth is actually grace.

Peter, the outspoken leader of the apostles, wrote, "But grow in the grace and knowledge of our Lord and Savior Jesus Christ. To him be the glory both now and to the day of eternity. Amen" (2 Peter 3:18). We are expected to grow. The Greek word *grow* is an interesting word. It's the word αὐξάνω, *auxano*. If you enjoy botany, you probably have heard a form of this term before. It's where we get our word *auxanometer*, an instrument used to measure the growth of branches. In the Scriptures it means "to grow up, to progress, to increase, or to raise position." In our spiritual lives, growth happens as we progress in our Christlikeness. Growth is not optional; it's an absolute spiritual necessity. If you could imagine the Christian life like riding a bicycle: If you aren't moving forward, you're falling off. Spiritually, if we're not moving forward confidently, we're not growing.

Peter makes this unique connection between our spiritual growth and God's grace. Grace could be considered the key that not only opens the door of salvation but also unlocks the pantry of spiritual growth in Christ. In other words, grace not only brings us the gift of salvation, but also the gift of our spiritual growth. This means that grace isn't static. It's dynamic. This means that grace is equipped to bring real change into our lives and induces increased growth.

Now as we consider this idea, I want to remind you who's writing these verses. This is Peter. Remember Peter's story? Peter was the one who said, "Jesus, I will never deny you," and yet what did he do a short time later? He denied Jesus three times. As a result, I believe that Peter understood the grace of God in an extremely unique way. Peter came to understand that grace will find you in your deepest shame, but it won't leave you there. Or an even more broad way to say it is that grace will find you anywhere, but it won't leave you there. To go from an outright denier to an unashamed declarer, Peter had a front row seat to grace's work. Grace has this incredibly dynamic ability to move you from life's biggest setbacks to life's biggest setups.

So how does grace become an immature idol? As we have seen over and over again, everything that makes grace so amazing can also make it somewhat dangerous. Have you ever felt stalled or stuck in your spiritual growth? I've been around enough to know that all of us have probably felt this at one time or another in our spiritual journeys. These stuck moments in our spiritual growth are exactly where the shadow side of grace shows itself. In fact, I would say that an incomplete view of grace is the cause of many stuck periods in our spiritual growth. Let me state it another way.

> **Grace becomes an idol when it cripples us instead of compels us in our spiritual growth in Christ.**

Could it be that when we get stuck, stalled, or even distracted in our spiritual growth, we can be secure in our salvation by grace, but we are hindering that same grace from taking us forward? We might think, "Okay, I've got salvation; I'm good to go. I don't have to fear the future. I know that I'm going to heaven." But we don't see any spiritual progression. This leads to one of the greatest problems that the church faces today, and explicitly most Christians...a huge lack of spiritual maturity. Too many people are immature and ill-equipped to handle the work that God desires them to do. Warren Wiersbe once described this truth decades ago when he said, "After over forty years of ministry, I am convinced that spiritual immaturity is the number one problem in our churches today."[1]

It's like the little boy who falls out of bed in the middle of the night and his mom comes rushing in to him, and she asks, "How'd you fall out of the bed?" And the child responds, "I must have gotten too close to where I got in." That's the way many people could describe their spiritual journey. They are too close to where they got in. They have salvation, they know Christ, they have been rescued by the work of God, but they stay right there. True biblical grace doesn't leave us there. Grace isn't meant to leave us at the door. It's meant to bring us into the foyer, the kitchen, and the living room where deep intimacy with Jesus Christ can be cultivated.

Grace that leaves us complacent, apathetic, or settled only leads to immaturity, not to growth. It's like using crutches when we are able to walk. We don't progress; we actually become more immobile. It reminds me of when my mom had knee replacement surgery. I had the distinct privilege of being one of her rehab coaches. I was blown away by how often the physical therapists wanted her to move, bend, lift, and walk on her leg. They didn't want her to simply sit in a recliner resting. They wanted her using her knee for the needed strength and healing. Many people view grace like a recliner. I've got what I need; now I can sit back and enjoy life. But that's actually immature grace. Instead of being the greatest resource of our spiritual lives, it becomes one of the most unused and underutilized assets in our lives.

---

1   Warren W. Wiersbe, *Be Mature: Growing Up in Christ*, 2nd ed., The BE Series Commentary (Colorado Springs: David C. Cook, 2008), 24.

MISCONCEPTIONS ABOUT SPIRITUAL GROWTH

So HOW DOES GRACE LEAD us to immaturity in the first place and what do we do when confronting the idol of immature grace? Believe it or not, whenever grace leads to immaturity instead of growth in our faith journey, it usually stems from faulty thinking about how we derive spiritual growth in the first place. We unintentionally approach spiritual growth with the following misconceptions:

SPIRITUAL GROWTH IS PREDOMINANTLY BASED UPON KNOWLEDGE

SOME THINK THAT SPIRITUAL GROWTH is predominantly based upon knowledge, and more specifically, knowledge of God and the Bible. They believe our standing with God is based upon our knowledge of God and biblical information. Consequently, this thinking causes grace to become a crutch that you lean on as you discover more knowledge but doesn't necessarily cause direct obedience. Far too many confuse theological knowledge with spiritual maturity. The problem is we don't just think our theology...we live our theology. Now, please don't misunderstand me, good theology and biblical literacy are immensely important. I mean, this entire book has been meant to engage our thinking concerning biblical grace.

The question is, if I merely know more about God, do I then know grace? The answer is unequivocally "No!" Second Peter 3:18 starts with the challenge to "grow in the grace of God and knowledge of our Lord." Peter starts with grace and not knowledge. You know why? Because Peter knows and agrees with the words of Paul, that knowledge puffs up (1 Corinthians 8:1). Just merely having knowledge about God doesn't necessarily equal spiritual growth.

I know many people who know the Bible much better than I do, better than most of us, and yet their hearts are far from God. Some don't even follow Christ. I know people who reject Christianity, yet they know much more about the information in the Bible than we do. There are also many churchgoers who have a tendency to say, "I already know this stuff, why do I need to hear it or study it again?"

Without admitting it, they think that by knowing it they have arrived. But the Bible itself talks more about applying its words than merely knowing them. Growing in grace doesn't just come from knowing the Scripture, but by intentionally living it. If we are reading the Bible accurately, it will move us from information to transformation.

SPIRITUAL GROWTH NATURALLY HAPPENS OVER TIME

MANY THINK THAT SPIRITUAL GROWTH naturally happens over time. They view their grace journey in the form of an equation. I don't know if you remember the simple equations from ninth grade algebra (if you do, you are probably in education or have an uncanny love for math). There was one particular equation that seems to fit this conversation: distance = rate x time. This equation gives us the solution to finding distance.

The equation applied looks something like this: If you're going 5 mph and you're traveling for 1,000 hours, you're going to travel 5,000 miles. Or if you're going 50 mph, it will take you 100 hours to travel 5,000 miles.[2] That's the equation…distance = rate x time. This is precisely the way many Christians describe their spiritual growth. "I've known Christ for twenty years." "I've known Christ for thirty years." "I've known Christ for fifteen years." And so on and so forth. They judge their spiritual progression on the basis of the quantity of time they have been a Christ-follower.

Now let's be honest, this line of reasoning doesn't necessarily mean that you're growing spiritually. We all probably know people who have known Christ for fifty years and yet could still be considered spiritual infants. They are poking along the spiritual journey, or even stalled. They have not progressed in the grace of God. Duration of time doesn't assume that growth has taken place.

Oddly enough, as I've grown in Christ, I have found there is actually a paradox of progress. What in the world does that mean? The paradox of progress says: "The farther I go along in my spiritual journey, the farther I realize I have to go and the more I want to go there." The longer I have been a Christian, the more I realize that I have so

2   Math teachers are more than welcome to correct anything mistaken.

much farther I need to spiritually go, and at the same time there is something in me that wants to keep going deeper and wider. That's the paradox of progress. I am not nearly where I should be spiritually, but grace is, ever so slowly, moving me forward.

SPIRITUAL GROWTH IS ACCOMPLISHED THROUGH ACTIVITY

WHEN GRACE IS USED AS an idol, we begin to believe that spiritual growth is accomplished through activity. Many Christians live by the mantra, "I'm going to grow spiritually by getting busier...by committing to more." You can probably guess where that leads. To overwhelming exhaustion and devastating burnout. Of course, I'm not saying we shouldn't be busy about the things of God. I'm not saying we shouldn't work hard, that we shouldn't go after spiritual progression.

James, the brother of Jesus, writes in his epistle, "Faith without works is dead." Work is a necessary outpouring of our faith. Or another way to state it, faith creates works and works are the evidence of faith. But it is faulty to think that if we just get involved in more activities, we are going to accelerate spiritual growth. In fact, some of the most immature people can actually be the busiest.

Ironically, you find that this type of living can certainly give you a spiritual spark, but the spark eventually burns out. It never catches the way you would want and, eventually, you feel as if you're merely going through the motions. I know many people who are busy with ministry, but slowly their activity becomes motion instead of a true grace movement in their lives.

SPIRITUAL GROWTH OCCURS THROUGH TEMPORARY SPIRITUAL SUCCESSES

MANY PEOPLE CONSIDER SPIRITUAL GROWTH like a vitamin. If I can just pop a spiritual pill every day, I will spiritually grow. They think that if they can just add another sound bite by a certain spiritually focused podcast, read a Christian book, attend a Christian conference or seminar, or watch their favorite pastor preach, spiritual growth will somehow happen. No doubt, these things are good, and maybe even essential, but they don't necessarily grow us in grace. They give you a great spiritual "experience," but they can fail to take you farther in your spiritual growth.

The reason this is faulty thinking is because it views spiritual growth as linear instead of organic, straight rather than up and down. Our spiritual growth is anything but a linear journey—it's deeply organic...it's not exact—it's messy. When we attempt to grow spiritually through small bursts of spiritual experiences, it can leave us stalled, distracted, or even dissatisfied with where we are on the journey. And potentially, instead of being a vitamin to enhance God's grace in our journey, it confuses the effect of grace on our journey.

It's like an athlete who constantly practices. Certainly, practice is good. But the only way to know whether practice is effective is to measure how you play in the game. Spiritually speaking, we can get small spiritual bursts through many different experiences. Ever felt more spiritually vibrant after a vacation? Of course we have. We rested...we reengaged...we prayed...we read. But grace does its best work when we get back to the grind. When we are faced with the everyday call to obedience.

I have no doubt that most of you reading this book have no desire to spiritually regress. You are probably reading this because you don't just want to use grace to get what you want; you don't want grace to be an idol (and ironically make us idle on our journey). No...we want to progress, we want to develop, we want to go forward in our spiritual lives, we want to grow in grace. In order for that to happen, we have to realize a simple, yet immensely profound, truth...there are no shortcuts to spiritual growth. There is no secret pill that can make us progress on our spiritual journey. It's deeper than mere knowledge, beyond simply passing time, more than sheer activity, and better than any experience. Spiritual growth has to be an intentional pursuit.

GROWING IN GRACE

So exactly how can we grow in grace? Peter emphatically answers this in 2 Peter 3. There are actually four main verbs that control this text. These imperatives give us clear answers to our spiritual growth.

> *Therefore, beloved, since you are waiting for these,[3] be diligent to be found by him without spot or blemish, and at peace. And count the patience of our Lord as salvation, just as our beloved brother Paul also wrote to you according to the wisdom given him, as he does in all his letters when he speaks in them of these matters. There are some things in them that are hard to understand, which the ignorant and unstable twist to their own destruction, as they do the other Scriptures. You therefore, beloved, knowing this beforehand, take care that you are not carried away with the error of lawless people and lose your own stability. But grow in the grace and knowledge of our Lord and Savior Jesus Christ. To him be the glory both now and to the day of eternity. Amen.* (2 Peter 3:14–18)

GRACE IS OUR INSPIRATION TO GROW AND NOT OUR INHIBITION FROM GROWTH

See grace as your inspiration to grow, not your inhibition from growth. Peter begins this passage by declaring, "Therefore, beloved, since you are waiting for these…" What are they waiting on? In the previous passages, he reminded them that they should be patiently waiting for the coming of Christ, the earth to dissolve, and for God to be revealed. As they were eagerly waiting for these important things to take place, he reminds them that they should "be diligent to be found by him" (2 Peter 3:14).

---

3   Immediately preceding this text, Peter gave details about the Lord's return. He is encouraging them to be patient in their waiting, but not inactive in their waiting.

Let me explain what he's saying here. The word *diligent* is the Greek word σπουδάζω, *spoudazo*. It means to exert oneself, or to endeavor. So why does this matter? I don't know if you are a member of a gym or not (if you aren't, there is no judgment here), but most of us probably have had similar experiences in the gym. For a long time, I was a member of Planet Fitness. You know, that place that calls itself the "judgment free zone." Well, I have to confess, I'm going to judge for a moment (don't worry, not you).

Inside Planet Fitness, the YMCA, or any similar workout location, there are three different types of people. Some are very serious about working out. Their workouts are focused and intense. They are clearly there to get things done. And their bodies prove it. Then there are others who are kind of in-between. They are there to get in shape or stay in shape, but they aren't quite as obsessed as others. They aren't bodybuilders but they care about their shape. I would consider myself one of those people (which may be my problem).

But then there is a third group. They are members of the gym who appear to be there to work out, but they spend their entire time fraternizing with other patrons. If you've ever been to the gym, you know what I'm talking about. They go from station to station talking to people. These folks spend their entire time in the gym acting as if it's a meet market instead of a meat market. They aren't there to build muscle but to socialize.

I would consider myself to be pretty perceptive, a people watcher if you will. And here is what I have observed…these people will walk around the gym, with a towel in hand (in case they sweat or probably more likely so that they can look like they are sweating), they will even lean on the benches and machines, but the entire time they never actually do anything. At the end of your workout, you go into the locker room dripping wet with sweat, and they walk in and say something like "Woo, what a workout!" Of course, you look at them strangely because you know they did absolutely nothing!

Day after day, week after week, they come into the gym, with no obvious results. Why? Because they aren't doing what it takes to make physical progress. They look the part. They are even in the right place but aren't actually doing anything to progress. That's exactly what Peter is getting at. He says, "Listen-spiritual growth happens when you and I willingly exert ourselves. Growing in grace is on us. It's on me-it's on you."

Just like muscles need to be developed or they will atrophy, we have to be willing to spiritually work out. Grace calls us into an active spiritual journey, not a passive one. Now what does this look like? Better yet, what makes a person walk around the gym but not actually accomplish anything? The answer is quite simple. It's because they don't have a plan. They don't know where they're going. They don't have a picture of what they want to look like, what they want to become. They go to the gym but return never looking or feeling any better. That's exactly the question we have to answer. What's the plan of grace...the goal of grace? What is the effort actually leading me to? Peter answers this question with the simple phrase "without spot or blemish." This is similar to Paul's description in Ephesians 4,

> *And he gave the apostles, the prophets, the evangelists, the shepherds and teachers, [Why?] to equip the saints for the work of ministry, [To what end?] for building up the body of Christ, until we all attain to the unity of the faith and of the knowledge of the Son of God, to mature manhood, to the measure of the stature of the fullness of Christ.* (Ephesians 4:11–13)

According to these verses, you can summarize the goal of spiritual maturity in one phrase: becoming more like Jesus Christ... conformity to Christ. That means our Christian life can't be static. It's not even a systematic belief system. Our Christian life is a dynamic manifestation of the life and character of Jesus Christ. That's the whole point of spiritual growth, that we look more like Jesus as we grow in faith. This means that we are actually in a partnership with God. Yes, God is faithfully making us like his Son, but at the same time, He is calling us to do our part.

Notice in Ephesians 4 it says "until we all attain." This is an absolutely beautiful concept. The word *attain* is seen throughout the Scripture. The root word is used throughout the New Testament to refer to a traveler on a journey who arrives at his intended destination. He knows where he is going and arrives as expected. It's like the parent who is awaiting their child's arrival home at an expected time.

In our text, Peter is telling us that we don't make the journey alone. Christians are not lone survivors. We're traveling with a companion called grace. As we are traveling along the journey, grace connects us to the work of God to make us more like the Son of God. That means that grace is our persuasion. It's our motivation. Grace is not our excuse; it's not our crutch…it's what makes us strive forward in the journey. It's our trainer telling us to do one more rep. Or better yet, it's the mom or dad holding on to the back of the bicycle as we learn to balance and pedal at the same time. We have to pedal hard…but our Dad is keeping us steady in the right direction. Are you coasting? Are you perspiring? Are you making every effort to grow in faith? Is grace what you're leaning on for salvation, or the crutch that is keeping you from moving forward in growth? Are you resting in the gym of grace, or is grace the place you're working out your spiritual growth?

GRACE LEADS US TO EXPECTANTLY CONSIDER GOD'S TIMING IN EVERY CIRCUMSTANCE

THE SECOND IMPERATIVE IN 2 Peter 3 describes how we grow in grace. Grace leads us to expectantly consider God's timing in every circumstance. Peter continues,

> And count the patience of our Lord as salvation, just as our beloved brother Paul also wrote to you according to the wisdom given him, as he does in all his letters when he speaks in them of these matters. There are some things in them that are hard to understand, which the ignorant and unstable twist to their own destruction, as they do the other Scriptures. (2 Peter 3:15–17)

Notice verse 15, "And count the patience of the Lord as salvation." Peter is making a fascinating point. One of the things that can cause us to struggle in our journey of grace is the slow grind that seems to define many seasons of our spiritual journeys. Many times, if not most of the time, our Christian lives could be described as a journey of waiting. It's irregular. It moves…it goes up and down; at times we seem to be moving at a snail's pace, or even waiting, while at other times it seems to be moving at warp speed. At times we're moving forward and at other times we feel as if we are going backward. In those moments we feel as if we are waiting, we can naturally begin to lose desire.

Of course, as we previously noticed, the context of this passage is following a reference about the Lord's future return. He seems to be stirring the question—how many of us think that it's going to happen in our lifetime? Most do. But the Lord hasn't returned. We are left waiting. But Peter takes this moment to announce that waiting isn't bad—it's actually an important part of our salvation. Now isn't that an intriguing thought? Waiting is valuable.

Has Peter lost his mind? Maybe that is the way it was in the first century, but not today. We don't like to wait. We want everything instantly. You could call us an insta-culture. Even Wal-Mart has given into our fast lifestyle by having curbside pickup. Order online and pick it up without leaving your car. Waiting is not in our vocabulary today. The problem is, when we do wait it tends to cause us to drift in the opposite direction. We begin to grow indifferent. We grow apathetic; we grow negligent; we become distracted. How many of us have felt this same way at times?

Our waiting might not be as focused on the coming of Christ, but we could be waiting on God for more practical things. I mean, why should I be impatient with God concerning his second coming when I'm waiting for God to show up in more practical ways in my life? We are waiting on God to do something more in our marriage, in our family, in our workplace, with our financial situation. We are waiting on God. Peter says to count our waiting as salvation. This season of waiting is actually profitable for his work in us. By the way, the word *count* is the Greek word ἡγέομαι, *hégeomai*, which literally means "to count, to lead, to think so as to grow." You know what he's calling us to? He's saying that grace calls us to consider God's timing in every circumstance and specifically count how God's timing is working our salvation.

Now I have to confess, when you first see the word *salvation* in that context, it seems like a peculiar way to use it. But it's important to realize that this isn't necessarily referring to our original moment of salvation. The word *salvation* is used throughout the Scripture to describe three different aspects of our spiritual lives. One of them is certainly referring to our salvation at our spiritual birth. But it can also refer to the process of salvation, called sanctification. It is similarly used to describe our glorification, when the work of salvation is complete and we become like Jesus. Peter seems to be most referring to the second one…our sanctification.

So he's saying to believers, "Listen, count God being patient in your spiritual journey as an aspect of development in your life." Waiting is a gift…a gift of growing in grace. I don't know about you, but personally when I pray for patience, I pray something like, "God, give me patience, and give it to me now." I don't want patience. I want an answer. But waiting grows our faith. Waiting is actually a part of the salvation process that God is leading us through.

Not surprisingly, this is exactly how Peter starts his first letter. He writes to them in 1 Peter 1:13, "Therefore, preparing your minds for action, and being sober-minded, set your hope fully on the grace that will be brought to you at the revelation of Jesus Christ." He says don't be apathetic. Know that the patient nature of God should create a sense of urgency, not apathy. A sense of movement, not a cause to stop.

So what do we do in the meantime? A few chapters earlier, Peter writes,

> *His divine power has granted to us all things that pertain to life and godliness, through the knowledge of him who called us to his own glory and excellence, by which he has granted to us his precious and very great promises, so that through them you may become partakers of the divine nature, having escaped from the corruption that is in the world because of sinful desire.*
> (2 Peter 1:3–4)

Christ has given us everything that we need! It's all been given to us, to grow in grace, to reflect Jesus, to live more intentionally for him. Of course, the natural question when we hear this truth is, "Then why does it seem like I'm constantly struggling? Why does it seem like I'm constantly walking with a limp, leaning in to grace and not progressing?" The reason is not because we're missing something; it's because we are not living in the awareness of what we have been given.

The Christian life is not "starting out" with Jesus and then "graduating" to something better. There is no such thing as "advanced Christianity." Every person begins their Christian journey with everything they'll ever need. It's not that I need to gain more grace. God's grace never increases, it's infinite. It's always the same. It cannot be more; it cannot be less. But what we do need is a lifetime to grow in the awareness of grace in our lives and in our understanding of the riches, power, and life that Christ has given to us. God's procrastination is not inaction…instead it's a demonstration of his work of grace. It's God making us more aware of grace's work. Are you seeing the patient moments of your life as a gift of grace? Are you seeing those moments where it seems that God has pressed the pause button as God calling you to become more like Jesus? A simple question we can ask in any situation is,

> **"Lord, how is this moment going to make me more like Christ?"**

That's grace. If we don't look at life that way, eventually it will become a roadblock to our growth and not the compelling force to our growth.

GRACE DEFENDS THE TRUTH IN OUR LIVES

SPIRITUAL GROWTH REQUIRES US TO defend the truth that has been graciously granted to us. The third command, found in 2 Peter 3, warns us of the importance of guarding the truth of grace.

> *There are some things in them that are hard to understand,*
> *which the ignorant and unstable twist to their own*
> *destruction as they do the other Scriptures. You therefore,*
> *beloved, knowing this beforehand, take care that you are not*
> *carried away with the error of lawless people and lose your*
> *own stability.* (2 Peter 3:16–17)

Peter knows there will be people in every generation who twist the truth of God, especially as it concerns grace. In our culture today, there are many opposing ideologies—none probably more predominant than *post-modernism*. What post-modernism says is, "You can believe whatever you want to believe, and I'll believe whatever I want to believe, so long as you don't tell me what to believe and I don't tell you what to believe." Basically, there's no objective truth. It's…whatever is good for you is good for you, whatever you feel today is good, just go do it, just live it up to the fullest. Of course, this is self-contradictory. If what I believe is truth and what you believe is truth and they contradict, they can't coexist as truth.

Of course, the deeper question for us is, where can this type of rationale lead if a Christian doesn't confront it properly? To a stalled and empty life. It leads to nowhere. People who twist the truth can lead Christians to instability and volatile Christian living. So he answers this problem in verse 17 with the phrase "knowing this beforehand." We have certain insights as Christians that are foundational and obvious. As a result, Peter is saying, "I know this, you know this, we don't have to be taught that there are people out there twisting the truth."

This phrase *to know beforehand* is actually one word in the Greek, *proginosko*. It's where we get our word *prognosis*. If you go to the doctor and the doctor says, "Listen, you're in danger of a heart attack. Your arteries are clogged. You need to stop eating fried food. You need to stop eating burgers. You need to stop eating french fries." Well, I got the prognosis. Now there are two options. I can say, "My life is in the Lord's hands. The Lord numbers my days. I'm eating burgers and pizza and whatever else I want." That's one option, and some will take that option (I will confess that if bacon was involved, this would be my choice). The other option is to stop eating fried foods, pizza, and french fries. I take the prognosis and now I make the changes that my life needs based upon the knowledge of the truth. That's what Peter is saying here. "You know this beforehand." We have the future prognosis. We know that there are people who twist the truth, so we better guard ourselves and not get carried away. And it's grace that gives us the security and stability in the truth. It forewarns us but also forearms us.

Once again, Peter invokes Paul's words in Ephesians 4.

So that we may longer be children, tossed to and fro by the waves and carried about by every wind of doctrine, by human cunning, by craftiness in deceitful schemes. (Ephesians 4:14)

Paul contrasts maturity with being tossed like a child in the waves. I grew up on the East Coast in Maryland. When I was younger, our extended family would all gather at the beach for summer vacations. As a result, I loved playing in the waves, bodysurfing, and boogie-boarding. This love for the ocean continues today with my own family.

On one particular vacation, two of my sons and I were jumping in the waves on a particularly heavy wave day. The waves were rogue and crashing pretty ferociously. We were a few minutes into wave-jumping and without our even knowing it, the tide pulled the three of us about one hundred yards down the beach. My boys described it like getting shaken like a ragdoll. We looked up and could barely see my wife and my other two boys on the shore. You could imagine the concern my wife felt as she looked up and didn't see us right in front of her. I, of course, wondered what would've happened if I hadn't been in the water with my boys. It pulled us so quickly and deceitfully we didn't even have time to realize it.

No doubt, waves make swimming in the ocean both exhilarating and frightening. You need a healthy respect anytime you're in the ocean. Combine this picture of the ocean waves with the illustration of children. Think about what children are like. They are impressionable, aren't they? You give children a balloon and they're like, "Wow!" If I were to hand you a balloon, you probably wouldn't be that impressed. But for a child…it's like a built-in birthday party.

Children are also gullible. They can be easily convinced of just about everything. For example, I remember as a kid being taught that you weren't allowed to swim until thirty minutes after you're done eating. And then I became an adult and researched this fact for myself and learned it's not true. It's one of those small lies parents tell their kids.[4] But as a kid I was gullible. I was scared to death that if I went into the water at the twenty-ninth minute, I would sink to the bottom and die. I was absolutely convinced! And then I learned, no—you can swim right after you eat. Actually, it's healthier to swim immediately after you eat according to some studies.

Children are gullible. They are also self-centered, right? How do they respond when they don't like something? They cry; they scream; they whimper; they whine. Paul says here, "Listen, don't be like a child tossed to and fro by the waves." No, no, no…instead, let grace be our stability in the truth. Let it lead us to growth and maturity, not to underdeveloped growth and immaturity.

Obviously, all of this effort put forth by grace is centered on the truth. That means we have to be people engaged in the Scripture. Now I know what you might be thinking. Read your Bible? That always seems to be the answer. But why is it the right answer? Perhaps some might think this is too simplistic to have any real value to spiritual growth. However, complexity is not a prerequisite for spiritual growth; obedience is. There are many truths in the Scripture that are simple to understand but obviously not so simple to apply.

Statistics reveal that most aren't engaging the Bible. In fact, studies show that only 19% of Christians actually read their Bible on a daily basis…19%! Just look up Bible illiteracy on the Internet and you will notice the trend moving away from a commitment to the Scrip-

---

4   As a parent, I have come to realize the genius of this rule. It gives parents a much-needed break from having to watch their kids swim.

ture. This is crucial because if Christlikeness is our intended destination, then the Scripture is what God uses leads us into a greater understanding and knowledge of Christ.

You could say that you can grow in knowledge without growing in grace…but you cannot grow in grace without expanding your knowledge of who God is and what he is doing. Scripture connects who I am and what I need to do with who Christ is and what he has done. And grace acts as the connecting point. That's why the Word is so important in your life. His grace is seen afresh every time. And when knowledge and grace keep pace with each other, guess what happens? We are safeguarded from heresy, apostasy, and unfaithfulness. Because knowledge keeps us from errors and grace keeps us in a loving relationship with Christ. One leads the way, while the other watches our back.

GROWING IN GRACE GUIDES US TO GREATER GLORY

THE FOURTH VERB SHOWS US where grace ultimately leads. Specifically, that growing in grace will guide us to greater glory. Peter continues in chapter 3,

> But grow in the grace and knowledge of our Lord and Savior, Jesus Christ. To him be the glory both now and to the day of eternity. Amen. (2 Peter 3:18)

Peter connects the grace of God with the glory of God. Most of us get this idea backward. We think that glory precedes grace. Let me share how I have personally gotten this wrong. For most of my life, I've prayed, "God, help me give you glory in whatever I'm doing." I prayed that he would increase his renown through my teaching and leading of his church. My desire was pure—I truly did want this from him. But I was walking in the lie of my achievement for his glory.

Now why would I say that? Take a look at the order of that statement. Certainly, God wants to get glory through my life and through what I am doing. But unknowingly, I connected glory to the result of my effort. "God, use my teaching today," or "Bless my work," or even, "Father, I give this time to you." Notice, it focuses on my efforts being a gift to God. That my time, resources, and skill are a gift I give to him for his glory. But it's actually the opposite. God is not glorified merely by my behavior for him; God is glorified by his grace for me. I know that's deep, but I want you to take a moment and think about this. In other words, God's grace is not a means for us to glorify God. God's grace is his glory fully realized.

I love how Puritan Thomas Brooks describes this: "Grace and glory differ very little. The one is a seed; the other is a flower. Grace is glory militant, glory is grace triumphant."[5] What did he mean? As I understand and live in grace, as I spiritually grow in it, what results? My life begins to reflect his glory. I don't create glory, I live in grace. And by living obediently in his grace, guess what he gets? He gets glory.

Let me state this with an important lesson I'm learning in my life: God hasn't given his grace so I'll live for his glory, he's given his grace so that I'll demonstrate all that he is in my life…which is exactly what glory is. I don't do the good things that I do to give God more glory. No…instead, I obey out of the overflow of grace. It's not, "I better do this so that God is glorified." It's, "I can't help but to do what is right because God has been so gracious to me." Big difference. Is God's grace directing you to greater glory? Are you attempting to give God glory through your efforts or by the reflection of his grace?

As we close this chapter, let me ask you: Are you resting on grace as the basis of your spiritual growth? Or are you leaning on grace in a way that's crippling your spiritual growth? Is grace propelling you intentionally forward, or is it holding you back. If it is holding you back, you're making grace an idol and you must reassess what grace looks like in your life.

I remember the summer after my freshman year of college. My wife and I had only been dating for a short time and were both selected to travel together on a Summer Ministry Team called SMUT (appealing, I know). We traveled up and down the East Coast, from Canada to

5   Thomas Brooks, *Mute Christian Under the Rod & Apples of Gold* (Lafayette, IN: Sovereign Grace Publishers, December 11, 2012), 170.

Georgia, serving at different youth camps. Our team would do skits, a couple of us would speak, my wife would sing, and we served as counselors for students from all over the different states. It was a tremendously valuable spiritual experience.

A camp we served at in Maine had one of the largest special-needs camps in the state. Most of the special needs centered on mental handicaps. There were adults in their twenties, others in their thirties, and a few in their forties and fifties. Yet mentally, many were at a seven- or eight-year-old level. Their bodies had grown to adulthood, but their mental capacities were that of a child. I remember being immensely overwhelmed in my small attempt to serve them. We would assist them, feed them, clothe them, help them get ready for the day, do projects with them, and make sure they got to their next activities. I have to confess that it was the most time I had ever spent with people with these types of difficulties. Every night that week, I would lie there dumbfounded by the idea that these beautiful people would never know what I know, never experience what I had experienced, and never fully realize the fullness of life.[6]

One evening, I couldn't help but transfer my thoughts from the physical realities of these beautiful people to the spiritual realities of many Christians, including myself: "God, is this how you think about us sometimes?" I mean, we have the greatest gift that's ever been offered to us. We have everything that pertains to a life of godliness, and yet our development is arrested. Our development is hindered. Why? Because we're resting on the grace that delivered our salvation experience, not allowing that grace to take us so much farther.

---

6   I would argue that they probably understood more about life than most of us. Their smiles spoke volumes to me. Their love for each other and the people around them was life altering.

NOW WHAT?

Read: 2 Peter 3:14-18; 1 Peter 2:1-3; Ephesians 4

Discuss:

1. How is spiritual growth modeled in our physical world? What makes our spiritual growth so difficult? In what ways does grace get misaligned, misused, and manipulated in our journey of Christian growth? Describe immaturities that you observe among Christians.

2. Peter compels us to grow in the grace and knowledge of Jesus Christ. Why do you think it's important that Peter describes them in this order? How can mere knowledge be an incomplete picture of spiritual growth?

3. How should grace be our inspiration for spiritual growth? Why do so many Christians seem idle in their spiritual journey?

4. In 2 Peter 1:3-4, Peter reminds Christians that we have everything we need for a life of godliness. Why do people who have been given everything they need continue to struggle?

5. How does the gift of grace remind us of our standing with Christ? How does grace guard us from error and deceit? How would you describe your spiritual journey with grace? What areas do you need to apply the work of grace?

Pray:

Take a moment to consider your spiritual journey in grace. Ask God to help you grow in the grace and knowledge of His working in your life.

Memorize/Meditate:

"But grow in the grace and knowledge of our Lord and Savior Jesus Christ. To him be the glory both now and to the day of eternity. Amen" (2 Peter 3:18).

CHAPTER SIX

WEAK GRACE

"My grace is sufficient for you, for my power is made perfect in weakness."
(2 Corinthians 12:9)

HAVE YOU EVER SEEN THE classic movie *The Princess Bride*? If you haven't...you need to step up your movie game because you are missing what could be considered a classic. While the movie came out when I was in elementary school, it became a cultural hit while I was in high school and college. Slapstick British comedy at its best. It also has many memorable lines that you will repeat over and over again. If you haven't seen it, it's a great movie for family movie night. For those of you who are now dying to see it, let me give a fair warning: spoiler alert ahead.

The movie is about a princess named Buttercup, who falls in love with a peasant named Wesley. The entire story centers on the tension found when Wesley ends up being taken captive by the evil prince Humperdinck, who is threatened by Wesley's interference of his own desire to marry Buttercup. Eventually, the captive Wesley advances from an enslaved crewman on a ship to the captain of one of the grandest ships on the high seas. As a result, folklore begins to grow around the mysterious identity of this great captain. He becomes known as a notorious, vicious, dreaded pirate under the pseudonym Roberts. Of course, he's not dreadful, nor is he actually a pirate, but that's the exaggerated story being spread about him.

So let me clarify...we have Buttercup, who is searching for her long-lost love, and Wesley, who is now the pirate Roberts. The story only grows more intense when Buttercup becomes forcefully betrothed to Humperdinck. As you can guess, as with any love story, Wesley makes his way to land and finally finds Princess Buttercup. Since she thinks he is dead, she doesn't even notice that Roberts is actually her long-lost love, Wesley (it doesn't help that he is wearing a pirate mask).

Instead of revealing his identity, Wesley decided to play a little game with her...challenging the notion that she would be engaged to a man (Humperdinck) she doesn't love. He asks her, "If you loved this man Wesley so much, why would you be betrothed to an evil prince?" She responds in one of the key lines of the story, "You don't understand the pain that I'm in." She then spits at him, *"You mock my pain."*

Wesley responds with this classic line, "Life is pain, Your Highness. Anyone who says differently is selling you something." If you've seen the movie, this is that great moment where she pushes him down the hill, and he finally reveals himself with the words "As you wish..." Which she immediately recognizes and promptly throws herself down the hill after him. It's an absolutely hilarious moment. On a side note, I made my four boys watch this movie recently, and they were like, "Dad, this is the dumbest thing we've ever seen." And that, my friends, is what makes it so hilarious!

PAINFUL QUESTIONS

WHILE CERTAINLY A HILARIOUS MOVIE, it's also a bit true to life. I want to repeat that profound line... "Life is pain, Your Highness. Anyone who says differently is selling you something." It's so true, isn't it? Life is pain. It's filled with stress, anxiety, worry, depression, difficulty, and trouble. We all know it's true, but how can we escape it? For Christians, the greater question is, what does pain have to do with grace? If grace is the greatest gift given to us, it's found in the world of greatest pain. And this gift called grace is often overshadowed by the reality of the pain.

If you were to label one thing in your life that has brought you the most pain, what would it be? For some it's a relationship. For others maybe it's parents who said and did things they should have never said and done. It could be a spouse, maybe a former spouse. For others it's a sickness. Maybe you've heard the dreaded C-word, cancer. There could be a myriad of other things...financial...the bank account doesn't keep up; emotional…a breakdown that you've experienced; or depression…a battle with anxiety and worry that doesn't seem to let up.

Whatever your answer might be, I can bet you that when you ponder questions about pain, it most likely moves some deep emotion in you. Why? Because pain does something unexplainable to us. Grief changes us. Suffering shakes us. And weakness leaves a mark on us. And the natural question we all ask when these moments happen is, "What is the connection between our suffering and grace?"

We have probably all asked at one time or another, "How could a gracious, good God allow this to happen to me?" Statistics would say that this is the number one question we would ask God if given the opportunity. I know this is one I would like to ask. The question of pain and suffering has been one of the worldly realities I have struggled with the most. I lost my dad at the age of eight years old, two months after coming to faith in Christ. I remember, after the news of my dad's passing, raising my fist in the air and crying out, "God…why?" I remember my godly mother tenderly saying to me, "God is big enough to handle those difficult questions. He might not answer in the way that you think. But he has great purpose in our pain." This same question is anything but new for us. It's the question that has been asked from generation to generation, ever since the sinful fall.

All throughout the Scripture, characters have asked this same question in many different forms and fashions. The topic of suffering especially becomes a major conversation piece among the first-century Christians in the city of Corinth. If you read the New Testament and were asked to find the city where the church struggled the most and Christians were failing the most, you would probably not hesitate to answer with Corinth. They were a mess. In fact, the word *Corinthian* in Greek means sexual immorality. That should tell you everything you need to know about them.

The Corinthians certainly had a unique perspective when it came to pain and suffering. Many of their struggles came as a result of a huge dichotomy found in the city. Corinth was a massive city known for its expansive temples and expensive lifestyles. Their impressive architecture, exotic living, and extravagant buildings defined daily life. In fact, if you're involved in home construction or real estate today, you have probably heard of a Corinthian-style home. These are homes with impressive columns and amazing detail, constructed to portray power and prestige.[1] The Corinthians loved power and prestige.

This description of success is probably true of most cultures in history. In its simplest form, success can be defined as exercising strength and influence. This means that personal worth is deeply connected to one's ability to show strength and wield influence. By the way, you don't have to study history to understand this. We see this lived out every day in our own culture, don't we? We use abilities, strength, and accomplishments to prove how great we are. Our value is defined by the sum of these traits.

Of course, this all sounds great until you face the call of an upside-down, countercultural life found in Christ. Faith in Christ changes everything. And it certainly doesn't lead to power and prestige in the way our culture would define it. No…just the opposite. For first-century Christians, immense pain and intense persecution were somewhat the norm. For the Corinthians, this reality led to some intense questions about their faith. How were they supposed to live differently in a city of great power and prestige when they were facing such stiff persecution? How were they to see the world in the midst of immense suffering?

PURPOSE IN PAIN

PASTOR PAUL, THE MAN WHO started the church of Corinth, who stayed there and worked hand in hand with them for years, writes some straightforward letters. Letters meant to encourage and challenge them in the midst of their difficulty. Difficulty that he knew full well through his own personal experience in his journey of faith and

---

1   One well-known home built in the Corinthian style…the White House.

ministry to the churches. By the way, this is true of all Christian ministry in general. It's filled with suffering both personally and positionally.

I know in my years of pastoral ministry, I have walked through many difficult things with many overwhelmed families. I remember the first funeral that I ever officiated like it was yesterday. It was a four-year-old girl who was killed by her own grandmother. Can you imagine walking in the room not knowing this news? I remember this desperate family looking at me saying, "Pastor, tell us why." They don't teach you how to handle that in seminary. All I could do was point them to Christ and the comfort and love only found in him.

That's exactly what Paul is doing in 2 Corinthians. Paul is attempting to comfort these young Christians, but he's going to do it in a counterintuitive way. He's not going to mimic the Corinthian culture that would say, "You have power, you have strength, you have success. Just name it and claim it. Just do it. You've got it." No, Paul doesn't follow the "Corinthian way." Instead, he comes to them from a very different perspective. He comes not from strength, not from prestige, not from power, not from boasting…but from weakness, from suffering, from difficulty, to try to prove the point that there's actually value in pain. That pain and grace go hand in hand.

Paul uses his own experience as an example of the value of pain and the role of God's grace in our lives. In 2 Corinthians 11, Paul contrasts himself with the power-play being used by many of the religious (specifically Jews) in Corinth. Their argument was the typical cultural reaction filled with bragging and boasting about their prestige, power, and status with God all because they were Jews. Like Rocky Balboa in a fight against Ivan Drago, Paul stands toe to toe with these erroneous leaders and declares, "If they can boast, I can certainly boast more."

> *Are they Hebrews? So am I. Are they Israelites? So am I. Are they offspring of Abraham? So am I. Are they servants of Christ? I am a better one—I am talking like a madman—with far greater labors, far more imprisonments, with countless beatings, and often near death.* (2 Corinthians 11:22–23)

Paul says, "Hey, I can boast about being a Jew. I can talk about the status of being a child of Abraham. Want to talk about success and prestige? I've got game." But Paul doesn't stop there. He takes it a step further by demonstrating the cost he had paid for following Christ.

> *Five times I received at the hands of the Jews the forty lashes less one. Three times I was beaten with rods. Once I was stoned. Three times I was shipwrecked; a night and a day I was adrift at sea; on frequent journeys, in danger from rivers, danger from robbers, danger from my own people, danger from Gentiles, danger in the city, danger in the wilderness, danger at sea, danger from false brothers; in toil and hardship, through many a sleepless night, in hunger and thirst, often without food, in cold and exposure. And, apart from other things, there is the daily pressure on me of my anxiety for all the churches. Who is weak, and I am not weak? Who is made to fall, and I am not indignant?* (2 Corinthians 11:24–29)

As I read this description, I can't help but feel bad for Paul. I mean, honestly…how could anyone endure this? He wasn't just beaten with thirty-nine lashes (the law only allowed thirty-nine); he received thirty-nine lashes on five different occasions. Notice the repetition of the word *danger*. Everywhere he went, danger followed. In essence Paul is saying, "Listen, I have been through pain; I've been beaten, I've been stoned, I've been kicked out of cities, I've been left for dead, I've been rejected, I've been assaulted, I've been persecuted…I understand pain." Could there be an even bigger understatement?

There was something about these painful moments that Paul believes was way more valuable than the power, prestige, and status described by the religious leaders of the day. To make the point even stronger, he asks two rhetorical questions. Both are found in verse 29. "Who is weak?" And the second, "Who is made to fall?" Or literally, "Who is tempted?" The obvious answer to both is, "I am!" "If anybody can say they've been tempted to walk away, it's me. If anybody has experienced the weakness of pain, it's me."

Paul is saying that if you could contrast anyone else's experience with his, there is no comparison. And he dares us to compare ourselves as well. Anybody been beaten five times with thirty-nine lashes? Anybody been shipwrecked multiple times and left in the water adrift for one to two days? Anybody been kicked out of a city? It would probably be best to not answer that one out loud. You're safe here though. Anybody been stoned? Not the kind that probably first comes to mind when we hear those words. But literally, stoned. We can't match what Paul describes. We lose the comparison every time. However, this isn't Paul's main point. He isn't attempting to draw us into a comparison game. He's trying to point us to greater truths about the purpose behind our pain, and especially how God's grace works powerfully in our pain.

GRACE DOESN'T EXEMPT US FROM SUFFERING

FROM A MERE LOGICAL POINT of view, it seems that God would reward those who do good with less pain. You would certainly think that God would give those in Christian ministry a free pass from pain. After all, wouldn't it make the most sense that the people doing the most for God should suffer least? How I wish this were true. If it were, I bet there would never be a shortage of pastors, church planters, and missionaries. Sign-ups would be through the roof and seminaries would be abundant. Of course, if this were true, Paul would certainly be the last person you would expect to suffer. But Paul is saying, "Listen, I don't get a pass from the pain. I've experienced pain in some of its greatest forms."[2]

The truth is, whether you are a follower of Christ or not…if you're an atheist, a Buddhist, a Muslim, or an agnostic and you just happened to pick up this book and you've gotten to this point… your background or experience doesn't matter. Everybody reading this is probably coming out of a trial, experiencing a season of suffering, or

---

2   By the way, if it were true that the most faithful would suffer less, wouldn't that lead to a type of paganism and ultimately idolatry? We would appease God by doing this or that only to keep from painful moments in life. That's exactly what many religions teach.

about ready to enter difficulty. We cannot escape the truth…all of us suffer. We all have people that we love die. We all have people we know who experience miscarriage and infertility. We know people with prescription pill addiction, people with closet pornography struggles, the loss of a job, children who rebel, cancer, sickness, and marriage strife. We are one phone call away from a bad report that could change our life forever. We know this, we all experience this, and we all have that in common. And Paul says, "I get it. I'm with you."

Now honestly, it's one thing to understand that we all experience pain; it's an entirely different thing to say what Paul says next.

If I must boast, I will boast of the things that show my weakness.
(2 Corinthians 11:30)

Did Paul lose his mind? Boast…in weaknesses? Think about the oddity of this statement. It would be like offering to help someone build something and saying, "I can't lift the hammer, but I will help you." Or saying, "Let's play basketball; just know I can't even get the ball to the rim." We don't boast in our weaknesses; we apologize for our weaknesses. How could Paul boast in weakness? It's because he possessed some keen spiritual insight into the answer that suffering asks…an answer to our struggle, in our strife, and for our questions…a deeply mysterious truth about the purpose in our pain and the hope in our hurt. An answer he came to know in a real way.

Paul begins chapter 12 with a reminder that he could continue to boast in his power and prestige if he wanted. He follows this with an unequivocal defense for why he could boast…because he had a unique experience of being ushered into Paradise. Now, I want to pause here. Paradise is an interesting concept. It's a word rich with historical meaning. Its significance is found in its Persian origin.

During the Persian Empire, it signified access into the garden of the king. Usually, a person close to the Persian king would be given a key to enter the king's personal garden and given the freedom to walk in the midst of the garden at their leisure. Because of this access, common people would get the chance to walk in the garden with the king. It would be like the president of the United States giving you a key to the Rose Garden outside of the White House. Upon taking advantage of your tremendous access, you run into the president, who decides to walk with you and talk with you. That's the image.

Later this word was borrowed by both Jews and Gentiles to describe heaven…the word *paradeisos*. Paradise is a picture of walking with God in the garden. Remember what Jesus said to the thief on the cross? "You'll be with me in paradise." Jesus promised access into the presence of God. And Paul was given this unique access prior to his death. Now we don't know exactly when this took place. Some scholars believe it was when he left Jerusalem to head to Antioch, which would be his last journey before heading to Rome to be put to death. Others believed he was referencing his conversion story. Regardless, there can be no doubt that this was an amazingly grace-filled moment. A grace-filled experience that could have left Paul with conceit and pride, but Paul wasn't boasting about this access. Why?

> So to keep me from becoming conceited because of the sur-passing greatness of the revelations, a thorn was given me in the flesh, a messenger of Satan to harass me, to keep me from becoming conceited. (2 Corinthians 12:7)

Instead of boasting, Paul was ushered into a season of suffering by a thorn in the flesh. Of course, this raises all sorts of theological debates. What was this "thorn" that he was referring to? Is it literal or figurative? What purpose did it serve? Unfortunately, Paul doesn't answer these questions in detail. We know it's deeply painful. He calls it a "thorn." The word is probably better translated "stake." Or even more literally, a "tent stake." I've gotten caught in a few thorn bushes before, but I can only imagine a tent stake would be much worse. We also know this isn't a literal thorn. He uses the imagery of a thorn to explain the painfulness of suffering. He further describes it as a "messenger of Satan." It's like he is saying this experience is so painful it's as if it's "straight from hell."

The description goes one step further when he says this messenger is "harassing" him. This word actually means "to torment," or more literally "to beat with fists." Whatever this is, there is no doubt it is tremendously painful. But it wasn't merely a painful experience; it was also a deeply physical experience. Notice he says it's "in the flesh." It's fleshly, physical, and actual. If this thing is meant to keep him from conceit, he can feel it in his body.

So what was it? I have to confess there are many different scholars with many different perspectives that fall all over the opinion map. Reformer John Calvin believed it was spiritual temptation; Martin Luther believed it was temptations and persecution; others believe it's some sort of physical disfigurement like a hunchback syndrome, epilepsy, malaria, or severe headaches. Others believe it was an ophthalmology problem.[3] So which one is the correct answer? Drum roll please...I have no clue. In fact, I would argue that the many opinions prove the uncertainty. Paul doesn't give us any insight into the answer because he wants us to know that what matters isn't what the "thorn" is, but what the "thorn" does.

The purpose of the pain in our lives matters more than the identity of the pain. And it can include all different types of pain. By the way, proof of this is seen a few verses after. Verse 10 stands as a summary statement for Paul when he writes, "For the sake of Christ, then, I am content with weaknesses, insults, hardships, persecutions, and calamities." The truth Paul is presenting doesn't just relate to physical ailments, it could be all different types of painful moments. It could be an insult. Ever been insulted by somebody? Offended by someone? Ever have words used against you? Your "thorn" could be relational. You ever walk through a hardship with a parent, spouse, or child?

Maybe for you it's been a sickness, cancer, or some other ailment. For some your medical history continues to linger like a "thorn,"

---

3   This opinion is based upon Galatians 6:11 where Paul writes, "I've written this letter in big letters with my own hands."

irritating life. Have you ever faced persecution? Or more literally, "scars"? Do you have any scars from things you have suffered at the hands of others? Maybe for you the "thorn" has revealed itself as calamity. *Calamity* literally means "a narrow strait, or to squeeze." Maybe you are reading this overwhelmed with worry. Maybe anxiety fills you as it seems you are being squeezed from every side.

Paul is saying, "Listen, it doesn't matter what the thorn is, doesn't matter what the suffering is, all of us experience pain in one form or another." For Paul, it was a "thorn in the flesh." It was painful and physical, and also inescapable. It was a constant companion in his life. What matters isn't the identity of our "thorn"…what matters is our response to it. The greatest question we can ask is, "How should I respond to this?" That is the question of all suffering, all pain, and all heartache. It's not if it will happen—it's how will I respond when it does?

This is where I want to pause for a moment. Can I ask you to take a few minutes and put yourself in Paul's shoes? Has anyone in Scripture faced worse for merely walking in obedience? Maybe Job in the Old Testament could compare. We would all agree that Jesus certainly faced worse. Nothing could compare to what he experienced spiritually by taking sin upon himself on the cross. But can you think of anyone else who has experienced the pain Paul faced for the sake of the gospel? And then, as if that weren't enough, he is handed a "thorn" in the flesh. A painful, physical, perpetual "thorn."

If we are being honest, I can bet our reactions to suffering like this would be strikingly similar. When confronted with suffering, our natural instinct is to cry out, "Why? If God is so gracious, why am I experiencing this pain? Where is grace in the midst of my struggle?" I think it's telling, humanly speaking, that whenever we walk through painful seasons, we question God's grace. Maybe not outwardly or publicly, but deep inside, we wonder where grace is for this moment. My friends, this is exactly where we find the danger and dark side of grace. As Paul describes, we don't naturally boast in our suffering. We boast in our power, success, and ability. And we think that God's grace only brings good things for our enjoyment and nothing more. So when difficulty comes, we look for grace to bring us an escape, to free us from the painful experience. And unknowingly, this is how grace becomes an idol.

> **Grace becomes an idol when we use it as a means of escape instead of a method of endurance.**

GRACE SEEKS AN ESCAPE

THE TRUTH IS, WE SPEND our whole lives trying to avoid anything painful. Anything that brings suffering, anything that seems difficult—we want to get away from it. Think about it, if you knew that you were going to face something painful tomorrow, wouldn't you do everything in your power to make sure you wouldn't have to face it? I don't know about you, but I would leave town in a hurry if I had to. This idea of escape is ingrained in our thinking from an early age. Remember when you were a child and you would get a little boo-boo. What were we told to do? "Go have Momma kiss it!" Get away from the pain or get rid of the pain, right? But then sometimes it didn't work. Momma's kisses didn't have their magical touch. So our parents would up the ante. They would grab a treat, like a lollipop or a piece of candy. Why? To distract us from the pain…to turn our attention to something enjoyable, fun, and painless. And usually, it would change everything.

I don't know about you, but I wish that worked for adulthood. Painful experience? Here's a lollipop! A season of suffering? Here's a Popsicle! That's how it works, doesn't it? We look for a distraction, an escape. And spiritually speaking, in a moment of suffering, most Christians look at grace like a lollipop, a distraction, or an escape. And unnoticeably, we begin to use grace to do what it was never meant to do. We make grace a magical "kiss" to escape the boo-boos of life. The problem is grace doesn't work that way. It's not a means of escape. And when we attempt to manipulate grace in this way, it leaves us feeling as if grace has failed us. Consequently, we end up responding in three human ways:

FREEZE

HAVE YOU EVER FELT THAT feelingless feeling? Have you ever felt numb? Like you can't do anything? You can't pray; you can't read the Bible; it's like your body's on Novocain. Maybe when difficulty comes, you go to bed. You take a nap. You sleep it off. Others run to an addiction or a habit. Ever heard the phrase "comfort foods"? Some attempt to eat their way through the pain. All of these are attempts to escape reality.

When we are walking through difficulty and the pain leaves us holding tightly to habits or comforts, how long does the relief last? Minutes? Hours? Days? The truth is, the comforts we turn to in this life are temporary. In fact, we usually feel even worse...mostly guilt and shame. These things may provide us a momentary comfort, but at the end of the day, they do little to resolve the difficulties we're facing. When suffering comes, many of us we take hold of our version of grace and we sit frozen by our circumstances. We don't know where to turn, and slowly we begin to question the effectiveness of grace's work. The problem is, we are using grace to freeze us instead of moving us forward.

FADE

FOR SOME, MAYBE YOU DON'T freeze, but you fade. Now, I use this word *fade* intentionally. Why? Because we are Christians. We don't flee...we don't run. We know we can't fully escape God's embrace. Instead, we begin to pull back. We slowly drift from despair to self-pity. We treat grace like it's our pair of sneakers during a game of dodgeball. When anything hard comes at us, we jump out of the way. We duck, dive, and hide anywhere we can find to keep from the pain. And although we know we have God's grace, we end up hiding behind it, and slowly we begin to fade away. Instead of "runaway bride" it's "runaway Christian." As a pastor, I see this all the time. People fade from the church. People fade from their community of friends who are able to encourage them. People begin to fade from Bible study and prayer. And unfortunately, anytime we fade from something, we fade to something else. And that something else is almost always sin.

FIX

FOR OTHERS, THE WAY YOU deal with difficulty is you try to fix it. Personally, this is my default mechanism. When difficulty comes, I attempt to fix the problem. Before I go any further, I have to confess that I am not handy whatsoever. When something breaks at my house, we call a handyman. But when it comes to the difficulties of life, I like to think I can fix it. In essence, we try to solve suffering like it's an equation. We go to God and say, "God, are you not gracious? Are you not good? So, God, why won't you get me out of this?" We claim the good nature of God (which is entirely true, of course) and act as if it's a get-out-of-suffering-free card. As if, God + Grace = Escape.

By the way, Paul reacts with this same human response. In 2 Corinthians 12:8, he says, "Three times I pleaded with the Lord about this, that it should leave me." I think it's important to note the distinction of Paul's reaction to this pain. Of all the pain he had experienced, the beatings, torture, and abandonment, it's this "thorn" that receives a vastly unique reaction. Paul goes to prayer. Now please understand, there is nothing wrong with going to prayer in the midst of suffering. In fact, the Bible calls us to it. Even Jesus prayed in the garden in the midst of the overwhelming cross looming in his future. Prayer is an important part of suffering for a Christian. But what stands out isn't that Paul prays. That makes sense. But it says that he pleads over this painful experience on three different occasions. The word here is the Greek word *parakaleo*. It means "to call alongside." It's as if he is begging, "God, help me. Come to me. Take this from me!" It's like Paul is praying, "You've given me more than I can handle.[4] I'm in over my head. I need out of this."

Paul is doing what many of us naturally do in overwhelming situations—we believe God's grace should rid us of the pain. That

---

4   This is one of the greatest Christian lies. Nowhere do we find the statement, "God never gives you more than you can handle" in the Scripture. In fact, Paul is proof of the opposite. I don't know about you, but I've been in many situations where it's more than I can handle. It's more than I can bear. It's more than I can take. It's more than I can carry.

grace is the tool God uses to fix our situation. It's the shovel to remove our difficulty. I love the way I heard one pastor describe our prayers: "God, show me your grace…pay my bills. Show me your grace…cure my ills. God, show me your grace…remove my fears. God, show me your grace…increase my health. God, show me your grace…plead my cause. God, show me your grace…and do it today." Can I be honest for a moment? If you believe that grace is the tool that fixes or removes your difficulty, you're going to be greatly disappointed in life. Grace doesn't work this way. Grace is not just the escape or removal of suffering. It certainly wasn't for Paul. Whatever the problem, it apparently stayed with him for quite some time, or even the rest of his life.

GRACE IS STRONGER THAN WE THINK

NOW PLEASE HEAR ME, I'M not saying that God's grace doesn't help us. But if grace is made an idol, lifted to a place it was never meant to be, used as merely a means to escape suffering, we're missing the enormous magnitude of what grace actually does. We are making it weak. We're attempting to withdraw from the grace-account instead of allowing it to deposit in us, and as a result, we will be greatly disappointed.

God might not always remove our situation. But God does answer. For Paul in 2 Corinthians, God denies his request but doesn't deny him an answer. He hears the request but doesn't answer in the way that Paul desired. Why? Because God's plan in suffering is transformation, not elimination. God isn't just in the business of taking pain away; he wants to bring purpose to our pain. And this is the true work of grace.

SUFFERING FINDS PURPOSE THROUGH GRACE

GOD RESPONDS TO PAUL IN 2 Corinthians 12:9, "My grace is sufficient for you." This painful experience is meant for something far better. Now before I go any further, I think it's important to note that Christians are not masochists. None of us are asking, "God, when are you going to bring me some suffering? Or when are you going to break me?" If you do, you need to see a counselor. No, if we are being honest, not only are we not fond of pain, but we can't stand even slight uneasiness. But if you're going to be Christian, if you're going to walk in the implications of the gospel, then you're going to have to be married to an understanding of the value of suffering.

As one pastor described, "We rebel at the suggestion of it, recoil at the sight of it, and reject the suggestion that it might be good for us. But the lessons of life are almost always taught in the classroom of suffering—whether you're 'suffering' through an elementary school spelling quiz, dealing with the excruciating pain of disease, or the heartbreak of grief."[5] There are lessons that can only be learned in the classroom of suffering, and only when a student is enrolled there can grace's true work be fully discovered. Suffering has a way of testing our values, revealing our commitments, and shaping our character. And we are students on a journey to discover where our trust truly lies.

And like a teacher giving the student the answers before the test is taken, Paul is handed the answer, "Grace is sufficient." Now I have to confess. I read verse 9 and think, "Sufficient? What kind of grace is that?" When you're going through suffering, grace feels anything but sufficient. But God is trying to show us that brokenness is in fact a blessing. That he is using our suffering to create something beautiful. How do we know this? Because suffering confirms that God's grace is actually at work in us. Let me say this again, *suffering confirms God's grace.*

The word *sufficient* here is the Greek word *arketos*. It's a beautiful word that means "to be possessed with unfailing strength, or to be enough." This is the same word found in John chapter 6, when Jesus fed the five thousand people (by the way, the five thousand number most likely only included the men). Remember that story? Jesus is teaching the multitude all day and realizes that they are hungry. His disciples can only find a little boy with a small lunch of five loaves and two fish.

---

5   Andy Cook, "Sermon: Finding a Purpose in Your Pain – 2 Corinthians 12," *LifeWay*, January 1, 2014, https://www.lifeway.com/en/articles/sermon-purpose-pain-2-corinthians-12.

After Jesus gives thanks, the lunch is served to the thousands of people. Miraculously, not only are they all fed, but the text says that they filled twelve baskets of leftovers. You want to talk about a doggie bag? That's the ultimate doggie bag. And the text says, "They were sufficient." God not only provided for them but also miraculously filled them. Grace in that moment was overflowing and overwhelming, and they were both satisfied and sufficient. The deepest need that we have in weakness, suffering, and adversity is not quick relief, but well-grounded confidence that what is happening to us is part of God's sufficient purpose in us. Grace isn't meant to bring escape but something far more satisfying.

The Scripture reveals to us that life is actually better with "thorns." Why? Because we get grace. We get to know the riches of God's grace in a way we could never perceive without the pain. What God does is he grabs the scales and says, "I'm going to allow the thorn, but I'm also going to give you a sufficient, satisfying grace." I love how John Bunyan, the author of *Pilgrim's Progress*, described this: "In times of affliction we commonly meet with the sweetest experiences of the grace of God."[6] It's one of the great ironies of the Christian life. Suffering makes us more aware of how God directs grace's beautiful work. It's like the old saying, "The shortest route to God is through suffering." This is seen all throughout the Scripture. "The LORD is close to the brokenhearted and saves those who are crushed in spirit" (Psalm 34:18). "The sacrifices of God are a broken spirit; a broken and contrite heart, O God, you will not despise" (Psalm 51:17).

I would dare say that God is seen most in our suffering. In fact, I bet if you went back and marked your spiritual journey, it's in seasons of suffering that you have had your greatest moments with God. Far more than in times of success and significance. This means that times of suffering might be one of life's greatest mysteries, but for believers, it's also the greatest revelation. You know why? Because we don't real-

---

6   John Bunyan, *The Pilgrim's Progress and Other Selected Works* (Green Forest, AR: New Leaf, 2005), 704.

ize that "Jesus is all we need, until Jesus is all we have."[7] And in difficulty, we see Jesus in a new light; we see God's grace in a new way. He takes our difficult messes and begins to write a signature message. He takes what seems to be the greatest test, and he begins to write a deeper testimony. Grace does that. The question we are left with is, how does this happen? How does grace work in this way?

GRACE REVEALS GOD'S ENDURING POWER

God describes how his grace works in suffering in 2 Corinthians 12:9, "My grace is sufficient for you, for my power is made perfect in weakness." Before we go any further, I think it's important to mention that the word used for *made perfect* in this verse is no accident. It's the same word that Jesus spoke on the cross. On the cross, at the end of his atoning sacrifice, Jesus cried out *tetelestai*, "It is finished!" "The debt is paid!" "The work is done!" It's actually a commerce term. In the first century when you went to a market and didn't have enough money to pay for your goods, you were given an IOU ticket. When you returned to pay the IOU, they stamped the ticket, *tetelestai*, the debt has been paid. It was a first century credit system.

On the cross, as sin was being paid for and shame was being covered, victory was being declared. It's an immensely powerful word and it's the same word used in God's declaration to Paul. Grace "credits" us perfect power in the midst of our weaknesses. A perfect power that leads to God's perfect plan to bring to us satisfaction and victory. In our suffering, we naturally equate our weakness with defeat. But when we suffer, we join in the same benefits of Christ's suffering. And just like the cross, weakness actually begets victory.

Of course, the logical question is, how in the world does that happen? When we receive God's grace in the midst of suffering, it is sufficient to give us stronger and more powerful faith. God's sufficient grace gives us sufficient faith. And sufficient faith plays itself out in perfect power. If this was an equation, it would look like this, weakness

---

7   Tim Keller, *Walking with God through Pain and Suffering*, 4th ed. (New York: Penguin, 2013), 5.

= grace = faith = perfect power in our suffering. You feel weak in suffering? Grace doesn't cause you to escape; it lifts your head by strengthening your faith. A stronger faith is then able to receive perfect power from a faithful God. But it doesn't stop there. This supernatural power does something that it doesn't do for anyone else across this planet—it causes faithful endurance. Do you know the difference between a Christian's suffering and the rest of the world's suffering? When we suffer, we endure through the power of grace. We don't escape; we endure. This is can be seen all through the Scripture. One of my favorite passages is Romans 5.

> *Therefore, since we have been justified by faith, we have peace with God through our Lord Jesus Christ. Through him we have also obtained access by faith into this grace in which we stand, and we rejoice in hope of the glory of God. Not only that, but we rejoice in our sufferings, knowing that suffering produces endurance, and endurance produces character, and character produces hope, and hope does not put us to shame.* (Romans 5:1–5)

Notice, as believers, we obtained access to stand in grace; the power of God's grace gives us the ability to endure. James, the brother of Jesus, shares this same idea.

> *Count it all joy, my brothers, when you meet trials of various kinds, for you know that the testing of your faith produces steadfastness [endurance]. And let steadfastness have its full effect, that you may be perfect and complete, lacking in nothing.* (James 1:2–4)

In both of these passages, the word *endurance* is one of the most beautiful words in Greek. It's the word *hupomene*. It's a compound word—*hupo* and *mene*. *Mene* means "to remain," *hupo* means "under." Endurance is the ability to remain under the pressure, the "thorns," of life. In the first century, this word described the process of placing a molded lump of clay in the kiln. When they pulled it out to check if the pottery was finished, if it needed more time, they would say *hupomene*. Let it remain under the fire just a little longer. That's the image. Endurance is the ability, the power, to remain under the pressure of life.

How do we do this? By pressing into God's grace. Not using it for our benefit. Not elevating grace beyond God himself. When we press into God's grace, we receive the power to endure. This is one of the great paradoxes of our lives. Weakness is a platform for divine power so that we endure when everybody else would quit. It's the athlete that digs deeper for the extra yard. It showcases what God alone can do in our lives. This truth leads Paul to write the beautiful refrain in 2 Corinthians 12:9–10, "Therefore I will boast the more gladly of my weakness. So that the power of Christ may rest upon me. For the sake of Christ, I am content." He is saying that he can now find pleasure and contentment in weaknesses. Why? Because in weakness, there is room for God—room for God's grace to do its enduring work. This means that the amount of pleasure and satisfaction you get in life will be proportionate to your understanding of grace's work in the midst of suffering. When grace is sufficient to you, you can find pleasure and satisfaction even in suffering.

Honestly, we can all probably admit that we are so drawn to grace that we use the word often, but sometimes we use it carelessly in ways that don't make much sense. Someone comes through a delicate brain surgery and we proclaim, "God is gracious." While no doubt gracious, if this is all that grace is, then it raises some difficult philosophical problems. What accounts for the fact that the brain tumor showed up in the first place? What about the person who dies on the operating table undergoing the same procedure?

We tend to predominantly use the word *grace* to describe positive outcomes and remain theologically silent when terrible things happen. I think grace is much bigger than mere positive outcomes. I actually wonder if grace is as evident in failure, struggle, strife, and even loss as it is in positive moments. In fact, some of the most gracious people I know are those willing to suffer alongside others in their darkest moments. And this seems to be exactly what Christ invites us into…His sufficient grace in our suffering.

So what does all of this mean? It means that suffering is not our enemy. Suffering is actually a friend. Instead of staring at the "thorn" on the stalk, we can see the rose that's developing; we can smell the fragrance of God's glory. I love what John Piper says about this: "In this season, don't focus too much on finding your strengths. Give attention to identifying and exploiting your weaknesses. God has not given them to you in vain. Identify them. Accept them. Exploit them. Magnify the power of Christ with them. Don't waste your weaknesses."[8]

You feel weak? You are stronger than you've ever been because you're weaker than you've ever been. How do we know that? Because sufficient grace is bringing enduring power…and enduring power brings lasting pleasure. Maybe we can't see it, but God is writing a grace-filled story of his glory in our weakness. I'm weak, but he's strong. And as a result, I'm stronger than I have ever been because I have never been weaker than I feel in this moment. That's grace.

A couple of years ago, my family and I took a vacation to the beach. As any beachgoer knows, one of the best things about the beach is swimming in and enjoying the ocean. One particular day on the beach, my youngest son, Isaac, looked out in the ocean and saw something shiny churning in the waves. He yelled out to me, "Dad, I think I found…the pearl of big price." Of course, I knew what he meant. He was obviously attempting to connect it to a biblical reference. I was kind of proud of him for his keen theological observation, even though he was slightly off on the parable. But nonetheless, it was indeed an oyster. So I reached down and curiously picked it up. We could barely see through the cracks of the oyster, but it did seem that something was shining beneath the surface.

As you know, pearls come from oysters. My son, knowing this, grabbed the oyster and loudly proclaimed, "We are millionaires!" He

---

8   John Piper, "Don't Waste Your Weaknesses," *Desiring God*, January 1, 2014, https://www.desiringgod.org/articles/dont-waste-your-weaknesses.

started talking about what sports team he was going to buy, gymnasiums he was going to build, and video game companies he was going to run. I didn't know whether to be proud of his entrepreneurial skills or scared that these were his thoughts. As I worked open the oyster, it was indeed a little shiny speck, what looked like the beginning of a pearl. Unfortunately, it wasn't enough to become a millionaire. It was still but a speck of sand in transition. But it became an amazing opportunity to explain how pearls come about.

Now, I have to confess that I'm not an oyster expert, so I have no clue how they think. I don't even know if they have a brain, but this is the process. What happens is a piece of sand gets into the shell of an oyster, and while the sand settles inside the shell, it begins to irritate the oyster. To the oyster that small bit of sand is immensely painful. It's suffering. So, in order to relinquish some of the pain, it takes some of the thin lining of its shell and begins to wrap the sand, almost like a web, until it becomes smoother. By making the sand smooth, it is helping its own cause. The problem is, without even knowing it, the oyster is actually making that piece of sand larger, and as the piece of sand grows larger, it actually becomes an even greater irritant. Instead of helping itself, it's actually hurting itself.

As the suffering increases, the oyster spins it more and more, until eventually this beautiful crystallized, clear white pearl overtakes the oyster shell in its entirety. For us today, pearls are found on necklaces, earrings, and jewelry of all sorts. The thing that caused immense pain and suffering eventually becomes something vastly valuable. How do you see pain in your life? How do you see grace in your suffering? Is it through the eyes of escape, or through the eyes of endurance? One is an idol; the other is truly God's grace forming something beautiful in you.

NOW WHAT?

Read: 2 Corinthians 11:16-12:10; Romans 5:1-5; James 1:1-4

Discuss:

1. Describe Paul's painful experiences (2 Corinthians 11:24-28): Which ones stand out to you the most? Describe some of the most difficult trials you have experienced: How do the rhetorical questions in verse 29 comfort you to know that Paul can understand our experiences today?

2. What have been your normal responses to pain? In what ways do you see grace used as an escape from suffering?

3. Why do you think that Paul's experience of a revelation of Christ necessitated a "thorn in the flesh?" What do you think the thorn in the flesh might have been? It says that Paul pleaded with God to take this thorn away. What things have you pleaded for God to take away in your life?

4. Describe how God's grace is sufficient in our sufferings: In what ways does our weakness prove God's strength? Knowing this truth, how should our response to grace and suffering be different?

Pray:

Pray that you would find God's grace sufficient in your most difficult circumstance. That you would endure instead of attempting escape.

Memorize/Meditate:

"But he said to me, 'My grace is sufficient for you, for my power is made perfect in weakness.' Therefore I will boast all the more gladly of my weaknesses, so that the power of Christ may rest upon me" (2 Corinthians 12:9).

CHAPTER SEVEN

STIFLED GRACE

But by the grace of God I am what I am, and his grace toward me was not in vain. (1 Corinthians 15:10)

M Y WIFE, ALLYSON, WAS THE first young lady I met on the campus of Washington Bible College in Washington, DC. As I was moving into my dorm, she came up and introduced herself to me. When I first met her, my immediate thought was, "Man, this is going to be a great four years, especially if all the girls look like her." She was absolutely stunning (and still is). Of course, she had the same thought about me.[1] Now we know that physical attraction can only get you so far. There was so much more to get to know. And so during the first semester of our freshman year, we began to hang out in the same friend group. By the second semester, a deeper relationship began to form. Now it's important to understand, we didn't go out on normal dates. I was a poor college student with no money. Most of our dates consisted of a Frosty from Wendy's (two for $1) at a local park where we would talk and dream about life.

Of course, as we grew more and more serious, it became time to meet the parents. Since Allyson was a commuter student from the Washington, DC, area, it was easy for me to spend time with her parents. Weekly, I would leave dorm life and cafeteria food behind to have a home-cooked meal provided by her mom, a fantastic cook. I don't have to tell you that these moments were more than just mere home-cooked meals and relaxing. If I had any future with Allyson, these visits were the serious business of impressing her parents. I knew if there was any potential for marriage, I had to win her parents over. And so, I began offering to do things for them around the house. This sounds simple enough, but Allyson's dad was about 6'1", 270 pounds, and not

---

1   Of course, this is based upon my recollection of the events. ☺

just normal pounds; he was an intense weightlifter. He was amazingly gracious but also tremendously intimidating.

One specific moment became an unforgettable memory. I asked Allyson's dad if there was anything I could do for him. And he answered, "Yeah, would you mind mowing the yard?" I have to confess, I answered, "Yes, sir, I would be happy to mow your yard," but, inwardly, I had a much different thought. Don't get me wrong, I would mow every day for a relationship with his daughter, but there was a deeper reason why I was hesitant. I grew up in a row house in the city. The amount of grass I had to mow at my house was the size of a postage stamp. I could have easily mowed the grass in my yard with scissors. We had sidewalks and an alley. I played in the street. That's how I grew up. But now I was expected to mow a nicely manicured, quarter-acre yard for the father of the woman of my dreams. You can only imagine the pressure I felt.

So, I get out there and start mowing, trying my best to make his yard look like a Major League Baseball ballpark. Full confession…I was mowing to impress her dad, hoping that the exquisite nature of my work would cause him to say, "I would be honored to have you marry my daughter." I'm bouncing around the yard thinking, "Man, I am in love. Just think of all the brownie points I am adding to my credibility." And then out of nowhere…the unexpected happened. All of a sudden, out of the blue, the mower literally blows up. The mower jumps about two feet in the air (no exaggeration here) and smoke begins to billow from beneath. I hear a cranking noise, followed by the mower shutting off-absolutely, unequivocally dead. And I have no clue what just happened. I attempt to start it again and all I hear is this weird grinding metal sound.

So I do what any great handyman does, I turn it over. Now if you read the previous chapters, you know that I am the least handy guy in the world. I can't fix anything. So I turn it over and just stare at it, hoping that proper posture and a little prayer would bring this mower back to life. I remember praying, "God, if you can walk out of the grave, you can make this mower start again." And all of a sudden, in that precise moment, God doesn't answer my prayer. Instead, he sends out Allyson's dad…all 6'1", 270 pounds of him.

As he walks out, I could see the look on his face. He is about ready to come over and with one punch drive me into the ground, never to be seen again. And slowly he comes over to me, and I never will forget this moment—he looks at the mower and proclaims, "Hey, Dave, it's no big deal, man. It's just a mower. In fact, I see right now that the blade is only bent pretty badly. It's an easy fix. Come on in and get a cold drink." I can tell you without hesitation, I saw the eyes of grace in that moment. Just when I thought, "Well, my future with this girl is over…it's done…I'm gone." Instead, I was shown beautiful grace. Today, my father-in-law and I still laugh about this moment.

THE BEAUTY OF GRACE EXTENDED

PROBABLY ALL OF US HAVE had moments in our lives where we have been shown grace. One of the unique qualities of grace is that it doesn't stop with the one who receives it. Grace naturally begets grace. This idea of multiplying grace certainly permeates the thinking of the biblical authors. As one scholar said about the apostle Paul, "Paul could not think of Christian truth and Christian conduct apart from God's grace."[2] In fact, grace is the first subject mentioned in almost every biblical letter, "May grace be to you." Because grace changes everything.

Throughout the Scripture, we see a beautiful picture of grace not only as the foundation of the gospel, but also gospel-centered causes. In 1 Corinthians 15, we see the evidence of this deep connection between grace and gospel. Paul writes,

> *Now I would remind you, brothers, of the gospel I preached to you, which you received, in which you stand, and by which you are being saved, if you hold fast to the word I preached to you—unless you believed in vain.* (1 Corinthians 15:1–2)

---

2   W. Harold Mare, "First Corinthians," in *The Expositor's Bible Commentary*, vol. 11, ed. Frank Gaebelein, 10th ed. (Grand Rapids: Zondervan, 1978), 439.

Notice the progression of the gospel. Paul says, "I preached to you the gospel; you've received the gospel; you stand in the gospel; and the gospel is now saving you." The gospel is not one momentary decision. Yes, it began at a definitive moment in the past, but it also is decisively developing us in the present. We see both justification and sanctification. The gospel has a progressive work in our lives. It doesn't end at salvation; it doesn't end at conversion; it continues to grow our faith. It's only when we understand grace's developmental work in us that we will see its multiplying work through us.

GRACE MAKES US WORTHY

PAUL DESCRIBES HOW THIS GOSPEL—THE good news that Christ died for our sins, was buried, and was raised on the third day (1 Corinthians 15:3–4)—came to him. He had the privilege of being personally commissioned to this gospel cause by Christ himself. As a result, he fully understood and appreciated his unique position as an apostle of Christ. Everything had changed for him. And notice what he says changed him.

> For I am the least of the apostles, unworthy to be called an apostle, because I persecuted the church of God. But by the grace of God I am what I am. (1 Corinthians 15:9–10)

It was the grace of God. In two short verses, he describes who he was and what he did, and at the same time how he could be listed as one of the apostles. As I read these verses, what stands out to me most isn't that he would be considered among the apostles—he was an eyewitness of the resurrected Christ—it's that he considered himself unworthy of such a position. Unworthy of God's gospel, unworthy of God's calling as an apostle, and unworthy of God's grace. This is the great apostle Paul saying this, one of the most well-known apostles in history. But the grace of God made him worthy. Grace changed everything. This is equally true for us. No...none of us can claim to be eyewitnesses of the resurrected Christ, but we certainly can feel as if we are unworthy of God's calling in our lives. But grace makes us worthy. In what way?

GRACE CHANGES THE WORST PASTS

YOU DON'T HAVE TO READ the Bible long to find a person with a messy past confronted by God's grace. Moses was a murderer, yet God used him to lead a nation. David was an adulterer and a murderer, yet God called him "a man after his own heart." Zacchaeus was a thief, but Jesus went to his house for dinner. Peter denied Christ on three occasions, yet he became the leader of the early church. Likewise, Paul says, "Listen, you can compare yourself to anybody else, but you have no clue who I was. I was the most unworthy of all men." How could he make such a claim? He described himself this way in Galatians,

> *For you have heard of my former life in Judaism, how I perse-cuted the church of God violently and tried to destroy it. And I was advancing in Judaism beyond many of my own age among my people, so extremely zealous was I for the traditions of my fathers. But when he who had set me apart before I was born, and who called me by his grace... (Galatians 1:13–15)*

You want to talk about your past? You want to compare what you have done? Paul says, "I was the worst; I tried to destroy the church; I was violent; I was a murderer; I sinned beyond explanation." Paul challenges us to measure our lives against him. Naturally, we all have these things we can look back on and wish we could erase. For you, maybe it's...

- You said something you shouldn't have said and you deeply regret it.
- You made a poor decision and it seems to keep catching up with you.
- A sexual past. Maybe even a recurring sin that you promised you wouldn't continue but you do.
- You committed adultery and you wish you could go back and undo the damage that you caused and try harder.
- Something you've done that's left you afraid of someone finding out.

- Your kids haven't turned out like you had hoped and you're left second-guessing your parenting.
- You feel as if you don't measure up and so you live in a perpetual state of failure.

The list could go on and on. Paul implores us to heed his story. "I was the chief of sinners...*but*." And this is a big *but*. "But the grace of God has made me what I am today." Grace changed him. This passage is a resounding reminder that our biggest sins are not too big for the grace of God. That every saint has a past but every sinner can have a future. Now you might be reading this and maybe you are sensing an overwhelming weight of guilt or shame. You know what I believe that is? I believe guilt and shame are gifts of grace. "What? How could anyone say that? How can guilt and shame be a gift of grace?" Let me tell you how.

In my journey, I have always thought that guilt and shame were God's way of judging me, God's way of pressing me down to feel the full weight of my sin. But you know what I have found through the Scriptures? That guilt and shame are a gift from God. Why? Because God doesn't convict believers of sin by showing us our shame, God convicts believers of sin by overwhelming us with the magnitude of grace. He reminds us of the cross. He takes us back to the empty tomb. He causes us to reflect on his work in our own lives. He tells us again who we are in Christ, that our forgiveness has already been bought and our identity has already been changed. We are then able to embrace the truth that God preempted our past faithlessness with his faithful work through grace. And as a result, guess what happens? Our desires begin to change. We no longer see the sin in the same light. We don't want to return to it. Guilt and shame aren't meant to merely leave us unattached and distant. Instead, these gifts attach us once again to the grace of God so that we see him afresh and anew, and as a result we don't desire to return to sin. Instead we turn to obedience. In essence, this is exactly what biblical repentance looks like. Turning from sin and turning to God's gracious forgiveness.

When I think of these truths, the first thing that comes to mind is the Etch A Sketch. Do you remember the Etch A Sketch? I was speaking to a group of teenagers years ago, and I held up an Etch A Sketch as an illustration. I noticed that many of the students were looking at me like I had three heads. They had no clue what an Etch A Sketch was. While I don't consider myself that old, it certainly left me feeling a bit aged. So I said it was "a 1980s computer!" Of course, they all burst out into laughter. Ironically, I think they finally got it. You use the two dials to draw a picture and then you can hit the delete button, but the delete button isn't a button, instead you shake the entire thing. One of the things I love about the Etch A Sketch is when you shake it, you literally watch and hear the drawing disappear. It's an entirely active process. The Etch A Sketch reminds me of grace. Whatever lines have been drawn in our lives through sin, grace shakes away what we've done and gives us a fresh start. Grace is greater than our past.

As believers, we can all agree with Paul when he said that grace has made us what we are today. When we look to the past, we are not who we were or could be. This reminds me of John Newton's tombstone, the author of "Amazing Grace." It reads, "John Newton, once an infidel and libertine, a servant of slaves in Africa, was, by the rich mercy of our Lord and Savior Jesus Christ, preserved, restored, pardoned, and appointed to preach the faith he had long labored to destroy!" This was Paul's story and this is our story. But if we stop the story there, we will greatly miss out. Please, don't miss the beauty of these truths. Grace does change our pasts. But if this is where it stops, we only have half of the story. For many believers, this is exactly what they do; they stop the work of God's grace right there. We see God's grace merely as our conversion experience, our salvation, and our transformation. We understand that grace has been extended to us, but it goes no further. As a result, we actually stifle the grace of God. And this is where grace becomes an idol.

> **Grace becomes an idol when you experience the grace of God but don't extend the grace of God.**

WHEN GRACE FAILS

GRACE ISN'T MEANT TO BE merely experienced; it's meant to be extended. It doesn't stop with us. It didn't stop with Paul. When we experience the grace of God but don't extend it, we misapply the true effectiveness of grace…we make it an idol. We are worshipping what grace has done for us instead of multiplying what God wants to do through us. Now if you reread 1 Corinthians 15:9–10, you can identify two different ways that Paul extended grace, but how we at times don't.

WE FAIL TO EXTEND GRACE TO OURSELVES

WHILE WE HAVE EXPERIENCED GRACE at salvation, we don't always continue to extend grace throughout our spiritual journeys. Many believers struggle with extending grace to themselves because of their own sinful past. They can't escape their past mistakes. I know I have seen this over and over again in ministry. Many look at their past as a hindrance to the future. I have met people who would like to disciple and mentor someone but feel unworthy to take the next step. I've met singles who desire a good marriage but don't feel they deserve it. I've talked to people who would love to make a difference in their community but feel like they are marked by their past choices.

We can wonder if at times Paul struggled with all the things he did before salvation, but we can be assured that he certainly came to understand that grace had an extending effect on him personally. The phrase "I am what I am" in 1 Corinthians 15:10 uses the present tense form of the Greek word *eimi*, "I am." Paul recognized that he was continually and presently who he was by virtue of the grace of God. He never lost sight of this foundational truth that undergirded and enabled all aspects of his Christian life. The same grace that transformed him from a murderer to an apostle was still at work in him. He was still being made new. Grace had to be constantly extended personally.

In what areas does God's grace need to be further extended to you personally? If God's grace could extend enough to save you from your past sinfulness in the first place, it is more than able to extend to your present areas of struggle. You are not who you were. No, maybe you aren't who you should be, but grace is progressive. Don't let the past hinder grace's progression today. Grace needs to be consistently extended to ourselves. But there is probably an even bigger way that we fail to extend grace.

WE FAIL TO EXTEND GRACE TO OTHERS

GRACE ALSO BECOMES AN IDOL when we have experienced grace but don't extend that same grace to others. How often does this astounding unconditional gift of grace become a conditional gift for everybody else? I don't know about you, but I do this quite often, mostly to the people closest to me. We think of grace as circular. "Well, I'll show you grace as long as you show me grace." Or, "I will give you grace only to the extent by which you have given me grace." Both of these thoughts see grace as give and take, and, therefore, it becomes tremendously faulty. Why? Because it's not grace.

Grace, by its very definition, means that the person I am extending it to doesn't deserve it. Let me explain it in a different way. It stops being biblical grace altogether when it's conditioned on some reciprocal gesture by the receiver. If we expect anything from the other person, it fails to be grace. And what ends up happening is that the grace that should be overflowing from me ends up being stifled. It stops with me. I've received it, but I haven't extended it.

Let me pause here for a moment and explain how this plays out in our world today. I believe this is a deep problem in Christianity. If you were to ask me what is the basis of most of our problems, I believe there are some deep-rooted issues that find their cause in our faulty understanding of grace. Where do I get that? Do you realize over the last decade that the population in America has grown by 11.4%? Yet in that same span, the church in the US has declined by 9.5%.[3] So, while the population is rising, the church is declining. In fact, did you

3   Nathan Venton, "The Current State of America" *Mission Frontiers*, March 1, 2017, http://www.missionfrontiers.org/issue/article/the-current-state-of-america.

know that nearly seventy-two churches close their doors every week in the US? That averages out to about 10 per day. There is not a single county in America that has a greater percentage of church attendance than it did a decade ago. To challenge these stats, experts have said it would take approximately 10,000 church plants per year to make up this deficit.[4] Sadly, we are the only continent on the planet where Christianity is not growing.

Why is this happening? I think it's because we are living in one of the most individualistic societies in the history of our planet. We are an increasingly individualized, fragmented society. We have compartmentalized our lives so that we are more deeply connected than at any time (through technology) and yet extremely isolated at the same time. Because of technology, the world is smaller. In fact, I'm probably not the only one who talked this week with someone on the other side of the world using video technology.

Yet, according to a recent study of 20,000 Americans, nearly half suffer from cases of loneliness.[5] Of course we know that loneliness is not just the absence of people. You can be in a crowd and feel tremendously alone. Because loneliness is something much deeper than the presence of people. It's deeply intrinsic. This has caused many experts to describe us as the "Lone Ranger" generation. You know what's funny about the Lone Ranger depiction? The Lone Ranger wasn't actually alone. Remember every time he was in need, whom did he call for? Tonto! Maybe this is a more similar picture than we realize. The only time Tonto was seen was when the Lone Ranger needed something. Telling, isn't it? How often is our feeling of loneliness based upon how people do or don't satisfy a longing in us or need we have? So often, what people bring us and do for us is what they mean to us.

---

4   Jeff Christopherson, "Where Have All the Church Planters Gone?" *Christianity Today*, August 6, 2018, https://www.christianitytoday.com/edstetzer/2018/august/where-have-all-church-planters-gone.html.

5   Bruce Lee, "Cigna Finds More Evidence Of Loneliness In America" *Forbes*, May 1, 2018, https://www.forbes.com/sites/brucelee/2018/05/01/here-is-more-evidence-that-americans-are-lonely-and-what-should-be-done

Unfortunately, our growing independence has also influenced the way we approach our relationship with God. We often view our spiritual journey as a solo pursuit. We all need grace. We all want grace. Then we are given the incomparable grace of God but fail to extend that grace to others. Instead, we create default mechanisms where grace becomes a bargaining chip in our relationships. Since life is all about the individual, we don't know how to make grace corporate. So grace stops with us.

Of course, this runs contrary to the Scriptures. In 1 Corinthians 15:10, Paul throws a major wrench in this thinking. He says, "By the grace of God I am what I am." But the verse doesn't stop there. If it did, grace could easily be manipulated and serve as an idol for my benefit alone. But Paul continues, "and his grace toward me was not in vain. On the contrary, I worked harder than any of them, though it was not I, but the grace of God that is with me." If we understand this verse correctly, if God's grace isn't extended from Paul's life, he would consider it to be in vain. That's a powerful statement. Grace doesn't just rescue us and leave us there; grace has to be shared. It works hard to accomplish God's plan. It's like an athlete who makes it to the professional ranks. They work so hard to get drafted, only to find that they have to work harder to have a successful pro career. Grace continues to work hard to produce gospel-centered results in others.

GRACE EXTENDS THE GOSPEL

GRACE DOESN'T REPLACE THE WORK of the gospel; grace extends the work. This is the journey of biblical grace. It starts with God and extends to us. Now it should overflow from us and extend to others. Grace begets grace; generosity begets generosity; grace to me, grace with me, grace out of me. That's the biblical picture. So what does this have to do with individualism? So many of us think of grace as the opposite of work. We think, "I have what I need in the grace of God. I don't need to do anything…to work for it…it's been freely given." Now we can all agree that this is true in our salvation experience, but it's not this way in our sanctification experience. Grace not only takes the place of works (justification) but also produces work (sanctification). In other words, grace motivates work.

Notice that Paul says, "The grace of God caused me to work even harder, to do more, to proclaim the grace of Christ." If grace is effective in its work in us, it has to overflow our lives. That's the point. This reminds me of what Paul wrote to the Galatians, "It is no longer I who live, but Christ who lives in me" (Galatians 2:20). Simply put, the Christian life is all about the dynamic overflow of God's grace. It extends from me; it exudes from me; it dominates the way that I think and act.

We could make many different implications concerning these truths. The Scripture says plenty of things about this. But there are also some important things that it doesn't actually say but heavily implies. In 1 Corinthians 15, I believe Paul is trying to tell us something hidden between the lines of his sentences. If it's true that grace should extend from me, then the obvious conclusion is that if grace is not extending from me, some major problems must persist. Specifically, I will end up controlling and manipulating grace for my benefit, which eventually will stifle or stop grace's impact. If grace isn't extending from me, either I am stifling it or I don't understand what it should be accomplishing. Either way, I'm hindering it. So, the big question I am sure we are all asking is, "How can I know if I am extending grace or not? Or if grace has become an idol in my life?"

GRACE EXTENDS TO OUR PASSIONS

IF YOU WANT TO KNOW whether grace is an idol or not, how does grace influence your passions, especially regarding how you interact with others? What are you passionate about? Do you view the people in your life as a means to fulfill those passions? Are you passionate about your family? I've done enough counseling to know that there are married couples who view their spouse as a way to meet their needs instead of a person they are called to sacrificially love. Are people your passion? It's so easy to see friends in our life as a way to satisfy some inner insecurities.

Are you passionate about money or work status? It's so easy to see coworkers, employers, or employees as a means to get that raise or promotion you have always wanted. Is your passion sports? Some fans use their passion for sports as a distraction from life's struggles. Is your passion the church? People can see the church as a means of getting instead of a means of serving. There are so many other examples of passions that could be mentioned. Name yours. Without careful consideration those passions can run amok. Beautiful passions can easily become horrible vices. Without self-control, passions can run wild and grace toward others can be hindered or idolized.

An interesting biblical case study of grace extending to passions can be seen in the gospel's impact on the Island of Crete. Paul's protégé Titus became the pastor of the church of Crete, a small island known for its piracy and robbery. In fact, there was a Latin proverb that described their character, "Cretans are always liars, evil beasts, and lazy gluttons." How would you like to have that on your state flag? *Welcome to Crete, where we're lazy gluttons, beasts, and scoundrels—come on in, buy local, join us!* If Las Vegas is "Sin City," Crete was "Iniquity Island"! As Christianity began to grow on the island, there came a credibility gap between what the Christians believed and how the Christians behaved. So the apostle Paul wrote a letter to Titus to describe what a Christian should look like in a culture where passions ran wild. Paul writes these words,

> For the grace of God has appeared, bringing salvation for all people, training us to renounce ungodliness and worldly passions, and to live self-controlled, upright, and godly lives in the present age. (Titus 2:11–12)

Notice what Paul says brings about godliness. It's not willpower; it's not guilt; it's not more knowledge or an inspiring message; it's grace. Grace is "training us" in righteousness. This word *train* described a type of staff that would be used to guide animals. This reminds me of many remote places in Latin America or Africa, where farmers walk their livestock along the side of the road, leading them from one pasture to another, all being guided with a small stick in their hand. That's the word here. Grace is the "stick" or "staff" that keeps us in line. How does grace do this? Two things. Grace directs us to say "no" to worldly passions and ungodly things that are wrapped in self. But grace also leads us to say "yes" to godliness and upright living. Grace gives me a vision of who Jesus is and then points me in that direction.

When gripped by grace you know how to live the Christian life. And this can't get any better than when it extends to my relationships. Many of us claim to be passionate about life. I know I would consider myself a passionate person. But passion without self-control and righteousness can go immensely rogue. Passion can be a quick road map for manipulation. That's why self-control and trust are immensely necessary for successful relationships. Those in our lives should see grace in our passions. That passion isn't just about the "what" in our lives but extends to the "who" in our lives. Stop and think about it. Are you living a life centered on your worldly passions? Are you living a life of ungodliness? If so, then grace has been stifled. Is there a credibility gap between your belief and your behavior? If so, grace has likely become an idol. But if belief and behavior complement each other, then you are living in the overflow of biblical grace.

GRACE EXTENDS THROUGH YOUR SPEECH

GRACE ALSO EXTENDS THROUGH THE way we talk to others. Paul writes in Ephesians 4:29, "Let no corrupting talk come out of your mouths, but only such as is good for building up, as fits the occasion, that it may give grace to those who hear." The Greek word for *unwholesome* or *corrupt* talk literally means "rotting fruit." Of course, we know that fruit rots from the inside out. We have probably all had moments when we have taken a bite of some fruit only to find it was no good on the inside. That's the picture. We are called to let no "rotten" word come out of our mouth but that which is grace-filled.

This reminds me of a time when my boys were younger, we had a family saying (a core value) where we would remind each other to "Watch your words!" When they were much younger, there were certain words we didn't allow. One such word that wasn't allowed in our family was *stupid*. The reason for such a rule was because we thought that some kids couldn't quite understand the context of "stupid." So eventually, everything is "stupid." Now please know, we are not legalistic by any means and certainly believe this is a personal call for each family. This was just a rule for a season in our family.

One day I was working on something in the garage and it just wasn't coming together. Finally, in a moment of intense frustration, I let out, "This is so stupid!" Only to look up and see all four boys standing at the garage door staring at my every move. Their eyes were as big as saucers. There was a gasp in their voices as my oldest exclaimed, "Daddy, you just cursed!" In their minds, this word was like the mother of all curse words. It was a good moment to teach them the context of words like *stupid*. As you can imagine, it took us a while to get over this moment. Now that my boys are older, at times they will walk up to me and look me in the eye and say, "Hey, Dad. Stupid!" Just because they can. Honestly, it still makes me cringe when I hear that word today. So why did I share all of that? Because, it's not about a specific word; it's about the heart behind it. Words are a window to our hearts. Our tongue is merely two pounds of meat. But that little instrument can do a lot of damage. There is great power in our words.

Proverbs 18:21 says, "Death and life are in the power of the tongue, and those who love it will eat its fruits." Words can create or destroy, heal or crush, build up or tear down, give life or take life. There is power in what we say. Words can become a weapon that slices people like a ribbon. They can devastate marriages. They can destroy children. They can wipe out churches. They can end friendships. We have probably all heard the saying "Sticks and stones will break your bones, but words will never hurt you." That is a big lie. We all know people, and maybe you are one of them, who have had their souls bruised because of the words that have been spoken to them.

In fact, scientists have said that with an instrument sophisticated and delicate enough, you could measure the sound waves of every word that has been spoken since the beginning of time because sound continues to reverberate throughout our galaxy. In other words, when we speak, it just keeps going in an endless wave. I'm not sure if it will ever be plausible, but it's definitely a scary thought. But Jesus said that God does keep record. Jesus said in Matthew 12:36, "I tell you, on the day of judgment people will give account for every careless word they speak, for by your words you will be justified, and by your words you will be condemned." Here's the point: there is enormous power in our words.

Are your words helpful? Are your words constructive? Are your words necessary? Are your words building up? Are your words extending the grace of God? Could it be that the direction of your life is based upon the declaration of your lips? This can equally apply to the direction of others as well. Consider your words. I heard someone once say, "May our words be measured in heaven before they are spoken on earth." May our mouths be a means of grace!

GRACE EXTENDS THROUGH YOUR RESPONSES

GRACE CHANGES OUR ACTIONS BUT it also changes our reactions. Our reactions are a key indicator of our experience of grace. The apostle Peter writes to a church that is being greatly persecuted by strong enemies. They were reacting in a way that you would expect. Some were fighting; others were complaining; numerous were giving up; and many began pointing fingers. Peter writes to encourage them.

> *The end of all things is at hand; therefore be self-controlled and sober-minded for the sake of your prayers. Above all, keep loving one another earnestly, since love covers a multitude of sins. Show hospitality to one another without grumbling. As each has received a gift, use it to serve one another, as good stewards of God's varied grace: whoever speaks, as one who speaks oracles of God; whoever serves, as one who serves by the strength that God supplies—in order that in everything God may be glorified through Jesus Christ. To him belong glory and dominion forever and ever. Amen.* (1 Peter 4:7–11)

Peter hands them a social admonition. "This is the way you should treat one another. Remember you are together as a family, a church." So he calls them to "keep loving earnestly." I love this word *earnestly*. It is the beautiful Greek word ἐκτενής, *ektenés*, which means "to stretch out your hand." It's like runners going through the finish line of a race. You stretch out, reach out, and do anything you can to obtain victory. Slide into first base if you must. He is exhorting us to love one another with this intense, do it at all cost, love. In other words, love uncomfortably. We live in a world that lives quite the opposite. We live in a world of extreme consumerism and competition.

This type of thinking can easily find itself in the church as well. Even unknowingly, we begin to look at people through the eyes of partiality and comparison. And without even knowing it, jealousy and bitterness can begin to set into our hearts. Sadly, many of these people have no clue we feel this way about them. When grace becomes an experience in our lives but not an extension of our lives, we begin to love people selfishly instead of fervently. And this selfish perspective reveals itself the most in our reactions.

Do you get easily frustrated with people? Do you "stretch" toward people or away from people? Grace calls us to love uncomfortably, to go out of our way to love the people around us. Why? Peter says love can "cover a multitude of sins." What does this mean? Kindness and love for others are the single greatest force for helping people to stop sin. When they see how you forgive. How generous you are. How we treat our spouses and children. When we are empathetic with one another's pain and excited in one another's joys, when we care for one another's needs, our love becomes a powerful force able to awaken people who are overwhelmed in sinfulness. This is the "secret sauce" of grace's impact.

Now this all sounds great, but how do I do this? Well, Peter answers, "Show hospitality to one another without grumbling." As I mentioned before, we live in a world of isolation and independence. God calls us to the countercultural life of hospitality, to welcome people into our lives and into our homes. Of course, this shouldn't be done with the reaction "Ugh, I have to be nice again." Or "Good grief, I have to host a small group!" No! He says to do it without grumbling.

In Greek *grumbling* is an onomatopoeia word, it means like it sounds. It's the word γογγυσμός, *goggusmos*. Take a moment and say it five times in rapid succession. It sounds like a gurgled grumbling, doesn't it? When grace is an idol, we grumble at hospitality. We see people as an inconvenience. People become projects instead of prizes that God is calling us to love. It's those moments when you see someone in the grocery store and duck into another aisle so that you don't have to talk with them. Have you ever done that? Be honest…we probably all have. What if God is leading us on a divinely timed appointment to encourage this person in our midst? Our instinct is convenience, not grace. And every time we miss these moments of grace, it falls short of its intended impact. As someone once said, "The generosity and love of the gospel on display is the greatest apologetic in our world." People can see the beauty of God's grace as we show grace in our hospitality.

Peter ends this section with a reminder to view service as a core value of grace. He writes, "As each has received a gift, use it to serve one another as good stewards of God's varied grace." We have been given the very grace of God, but it comes out differently in each of our lives. It extends in different ways through our gifts of serving. Notice the word *varied*. It's where we get our word *polka-dot*. This paints a two-sided picture. On one side, we each have varying spiritual gifts to serve one another. And we can celebrate these differences as a gift from God. But it goes deeper than that.

Notice again the connection between our gift and God's grace. Not only are our gifts different, but grace itself also varies. While grace came to us all in the same way, it extends from us differently. It overflows from us in different contexts, shapes, sizes, colors, and forms. For some, we need more grace to serve in our marriages. For others, it's more grace for our kids. For some, it's more grace toward our coworkers, family, or friends. Maybe for you it's grace to fellow believers in the church or dare I say, a pastor. For a few, it might even be grace for an enemy.

Whatever the context might be, we have a natural tendency to respond to the situations that need the most grace by using our gifts to serve ourselves…even defend ourselves. But since grace serves in various "polka-dot" forms and fashions, it should be applied in each context uniquely. Just as we did not determine, deserve, or earn our "gift." Thus it's a gift. How much more should it be true of the people in our lives? They may not deserve it, but we are called to extend our gift of grace.

Let me take it one step further—what we do with our "gift" says everything about how we think about not only the "gift" but also the Gift-Giver. It demonstrates our view and value of God himself. This means when that spouse says something they shouldn't, how should you extend grace? That boss is frustrating you, what does grace do? Your friend is annoying you, how does grace direct your response? Time after time, we will face moments that demand a reaction. In what ways does grace need to extend in your responses today? What are the areas right now that grace is calling you to serve? Let grace extend in your responses.

You know what's interesting about grace? We all want what it provides, don't we? We all want grace extended to us. The struggle is when that grace calls us to "stretch out" to the people around us who are most undeserving and ungracious. In that moment our nature might be to stop grace. To stifle it, hinder it, and hold it back for us alone. But grace doesn't stop; otherwise it's not grace.

So, if grace isn't working through you, then one of two things is true: you haven't experienced the grace of God or you aren't extending the grace of God. You would do well to ask yourself the question, *Am I extending grace or stopping its impact?* Are you loving people selfishly instead of fervently? Are you serving people willingly or with grumbling? How are your responses to the people around you? How do you talk? How do you react? Where are your passions? The essence of grace changes everything—our actions, responses, and words. These are the things that make Christianity and the church most attractive. Or let me state it another way, we become most appealing when grace is most apparent. We have the assigned task of exposing our neighbors, workplaces, schools, communities, cities, states, and world to the grace of God. May we not merely experience God's grace...but may we extend it.

NOW WHAT?

Read: 1 Corinthians 15:1-11; Galatians 1:13-15; Titus 2:11-12;
1 Peter 4:7-11

Discuss:

1. Paul describes his salvation experience in 1 Corinthians 15:8-10. In what ways is your experience with God's grace at salvation similar to Paul's? Are there any differences?

2. Why was God's grace toward Paul not in vain (1 Corinthians 15:10)? How should our experience with God's grace motivate extending God's grace to others? Why is it so difficult to show grace to other people? What hinders us from showing grace to others?

3. If Paul was relying on God's grace (1 Corinthians 15:10), why did he work harder than anyone? Based on 1 Corinthians 15:9–10, how does God's grace relate to our effort in the Christian life?

4. Grace changes everything. If you evaluated how grace is extended through your passions, speech, and responses, which would be most difficult for you? Why? How can grace bring change in that specific area of your life?

Pray:

Pray that your awareness of grace's work in your life would be so evident that it would overflow in your interactions with others.

Memorize/Meditate:

"But by the grace of God I am what I am, and his grace toward me was not in vain. On the contrary, I worked harder than any of them, though it was not I, but the grace of God that is with me" (1 Corinthians 15:10).

CHAPTER EIGHT

UNFINISHED GRACE

See to it that no one fails to obtain the grace of God... (Hebrews 12:15)

W E CAN ALL ATTEST THAT there are many critical and unforget-table moments in life. As I have shared, Allyson and I met and married while still in college. We had our firstborn one month before my college graduation, our second son less than a year later, and our third son a couple of years after that (and a couple of years later we added our fourth). Let me put this in perspective: we had three children in a little over three and a half years. You are probably thinking, wow you guys moved quickly. I blame my wife of course. She couldn't keep her hands off of me. All that said, here we were twenty-five years old with three children, living in the expensive Washington, DC, suburbs, with an entry-level ministry position. Needless to say, we couldn't afford much. And any extra money was used to buy diapers. Truthfully, Huggies stockholders owe me.

As you can imagine, going from two of us to a family of five in a few years changed everything. One item that we desperately needed in order to function best was a family vehicle. Up until this point, we had two small compact cars. With three car seats and diaper bags, none of these options provided enough space for us to go anywhere together. This was a crucial moment for the growth of our family. Of course, I had to come to the realization that this meant we had to resign ourselves to the dreaded minivan. The one vehicle no one wants to drive at twenty-five years old.

Allyson and I joined together in prayer over this need. "God, by your hand of grace, we desperately need you to provide a family vehicle. I will gladly take a Mustang, but I know we need a minivan...and an affordable one at that." As Christians, we knew that faithful prayer must be followed by faithful obedience. So we put the word out that we were looking for affordable used minivans. A few weeks later, my sister reached out to us to share that she had a coworker who was willing to sell their minivan for a few hundred dollars. I've got to admit, we were thrilled. My sister worked for the Department of Energy. We logically assumed that this would be an older but well-kept van. The only question I asked was, "Does it run and is it safe?" So we scrounged up all the money we could and decided to buy it sight unseen.

I remember the journey to pick up the van well. As I was riding the metro train to the location of the pickup, I was overwhelmed with excitement and gratitude for the provision of God. I was on cloud nine to say the least. As I arrived at the stop, I got out to meet my sister and her coworker. And there it was…the longed for, prayed over, desperately needed van. And I have to confess my heart gasped. This van was the ugliest vehicle I had ever seen. It was like one big piece of rust. It was a barely noticeable blue van, with rust covering it from the inside out.

I reluctantly wrote out the check and handed it over, climbed into my "new" vehicle, and began my embarrassing drive around the Washington, DC, beltway toward home. As I was driving home, I decided to have a little "honest" conversation with God. "God, are you serious? I thought you were a gracious God. Why wouldn't you provide a better van than this? Maybe I should have prayed for a more specific van instead of this embarrassing piece of junk!"

My complaint session with God lasted my entire drive home. Upon my arrival, I was deeply embarrassed to even show my dear wife and kids the van. But trying to be upbeat, I went inside and invited Allyson and the boys to come take a little ride. So we grabbed the car seats and jumped into our "new" family vehicle. As we began our little drive, my boys began shouting some astonishing words that pierced my soul deeply. "Daddy, can you believe our new van. It's so awesome!" In that moment, I swallowed hard, realizing that God was speaking loudly through my boys. And can I confess, for the years that we drove that van, every time my boys got into the van, they described it as the "new van." Every single time. While everybody else was staring, they were thrilled. Of course, we realized that they didn't know any better. It was the only van they had ever ridden in up until this point. But they quickly understood something that I came to know: this van was a gift from God.

WHEN GRACE FALLS SHORT

BELIEVE IT OR NOT, MY experience with our van is exactly the way many of us feel about grace. We understand that salvation comes by grace alone, we know that grace is sufficient for all things in our lives, we know that eventually grace will deliver us to Christlikeness, but in the meantime we are left yearning for more. Our search just seems to continue. And worse, we can grow stagnant living in the here and now. While we know Christ, we feel as if we are in the waiting room of life, expecting the door to open to a better life soon. In the meantime we can begin, without even knowing it, to look at grace as if it's old and rusty.

That's what this book has been about, the danger of reducing God's grace to merely an event that assures our eternal destiny and nothing more. To take the concept of "grace," add some eschatological language to it, mix it up, and think that's all that grace is. Now please don't misunderstand me, I know that God's grace leading us to our eternal home is an absolutely beautiful and necessary truth. But if it stops there, it becomes a diluted grace that has merely altered our standing with God without affecting our state for God. We can all agree that grace is supposed to be life changing, radical, and amazing, but if our understanding of it stops there, we need to spend more time standing in the aisle and staring at it. Because, if we aren't careful, the grace that is supposed to move us forward actually ends up holding us back.

Grace is so much more. Yes, it's deeply monumental, but it's equally developmental. All throughout the Scripture, we see that what it begins, it finishes. Or to say it another way, grace will see us through. Biblical grace is never halfway grace. One place we see this strikingly illustrated is in the book of Hebrews. In fact, Hebrews 11 is one of my favorite chapters in the Bible. It's considered the *Hall of Faith* chapter because it lists biblical characters who walked the journey of faith well. These people demonstrated faith in spite of their difficult circumstances and unexplainable results. One of the most curious parts of Hebrews 11 is how the chapter ends:

And what more shall I say? For time would fail me to tell of Gideon, Barak, Samson, Jephthah, of David and Samuel and the prophets—who through faith conquered kingdoms, enforced justice, obtained promises, stopped the mouths of lions, quenched the power of fire, escaped the edge of the sword, were made strong out of weakness, became mighty in war, put foreign armies to flight. Women received back their dead by resurrection. Some were tortured, refusing to accept release, so that they might rise again to a better life. Others suffered mocking and flogging, and even chains and imprisonment. They were stoned, they were sawn in two, they were killed with the sword. They went about in skins of sheep and goats, destitute, afflicted, mistreated... And all these, though commended through their faith, did not receive what was promised. (Hebrews 11:32–37, 39)

Notice the contrast. Some, through faith, conquered king-doms, defeated enemies, and the ultimate experience, received a dead child back to life. But right in the middle of verse 35, it continues with what seems to be no thought concerning the dynamics of the contrast: were tortured, beaten, and killed. Remarkably enough, this is some-what the rhythm and essence of our faith. For some, life will lead us to mountaintop experiences and glorious moments. For others, life will take us through overwhelming valleys and immense difficulties. For most of us, it will include both hills and valleys. Whichever side is be-ing experienced, faith becomes the crucial element that allows us to fully enjoy what life is giving or to downright endure what life is taking.

The big question we are left asking is, "How can we fully enjoy the beauty of life and at the same time be assured our faith will stand in the difficult seasons?" The author of Hebrews answers this question in chapter 12.

Therefore, [since there are these people with faith, and since faith is trusting God, no matter what], since we are surrounded by so great a cloud of witnesses [those who have already walked this journey of faith], let us also lay aside every weight, and sin which clings so closely, and let us run with endurance the race that is set before us, looking to Jesus, the founder and perfecter of our faith, who for the joy that was set before him endured the cross, despising the shame, and is seated at the right hand of the throne of God. (Hebrews 12:1–2)

The author uses race language to describe our faith journey. We are all in a race and we are running for a prize. How do we finish the race well? We look to Jesus, the trailblazer, who initiated our faith and will complete our faith. Now, if we're being honest, most of us recognize that God is both the originator and perfecter of our faith. It's the only way our faith could be effective. The problem lies in the land in between. We have come to know Christ, yet we are waiting for Christlikeness to come. And much of the time we have left on earth can be more like a desert dwelling rather than life in the Promised Land. This transitional period can be filled with dark and difficult seasons. It's like sitting in the waiting room anticipating a much-needed surgery. Anxiety can be high and concern can be great. For this reason, the author of Hebrews is writing to remind and encourage us to continue running the race of this journey of faith.

We are told to set our sights on Jesus, our pacesetter. When my oldest son was in high school, he ran on the cross-country team. I had little experience with cross-country before this experience. My view up until that point was that it was just a bunch of runners who got out to run as fast as possible for what was in essence a 5k. But as I gained more knowledge about how cross-country worked, I realized that there was a lot more strategy than expected. Because it wasn't enough to win the race personally, you also had to consider where your team finished. It was more of a team event than I could have ever imagined. As a result, some of the teams had runners who would attempt to set the pace for the rest of the team. To use the strength and ability of one to help the others finish stronger. That's the picture of Hebrews 12. Jesus is our pacesetter. He is showing us how it looks to run the race with endurance. So what did it look like for him?

Consider him who endured from sinners such hostility against himself, so that you may not grow weary or fainthearted. In your struggle against sin you have not yet resisted to the point of shedding your blood. And have you forgotten the exhortation that addresses you as sons? "My son, do not regard lightly the discipline of the Lord, nor be weary when reproved by him. For the Lord disciplines the one he loves, and chastises every son whom he receives." It is for discipline that you have to endure. God is treating you as sons. For what son is there whom his father does not discipline?... For the moment all discipline seems painful rather than pleasant, but later it yields the peaceful fruit of righteousness to those who have been trained by it. (Hebrews 12:3–7, 11)

Jesus ran this race and guess what? It wasn't easy for him either. He had to equally endure. Many people want to follow Christ, but it's not the easy journey we think it should be. Pressure to conform, difficult seasons, overwhelming circumstances, painful experiences, and staggering temptations can make our glorious journey with Christ downright messy. These moments can cause us to walk along the path, reluctantly at times. All through the Bible, we see character after character who were at times hesitant (from Moses to David, from Jonah to Jeremiah, from the disciples to you and me). That's why we are called to look to Jesus. He felt the weight of the pressures of life on earth but endured them. But how in the world did he do it? How could Jesus endure what only he experienced? Because He was disciplined regarding his purpose.

DISCIPLINE FOR THE JOURNEY

NOTICE THE BEAUTIFUL CHANGE OF language in these verses. It goes from a track coach saying, "Run the race!" to a father declaring, "I am correcting your course because I love you!" He is saying, "Don't you realize that the difficult things you will walk through in this life are actually meant to guide you in this journey of faith?" God is being a good, good Father in this moment. How? By building discipline in us. He not only founded our faith and will perfect our faith, but in this time in between, he is building our faith through discipline. Why? Because we, unlike Jesus, tend to stray. That's why the Bible uses the illustration of sheep to describe believers. Like sheep, we tend to get lost roaming in the pastures of life. Likewise, in our earthly form, we don't naturally stay the course. We get distracted from our intended direction. As stressful moments come, our natural step is usually a step away. So God uses discipline to keep us going in the right direction.

Let's be honest, we don't like the word *discipline*, do we? When most of us hear this word, a small part of us probably shudders in fear. The problem with discipline lies in our view of the value it has in our lives. What's the first thing that comes to mind when you think of the word *discipline*? Most of us, when we think of the word *discipline*, think of the concept of punishment, don't we? In our minds, discipline is what you get when you're unruly or disruptive. I know this is true in my mind. As a youth, I was the victim of discipline many times. My tremendously kind, sweet mother could turn into a firm drill sergeant as a result of something I did. And I have to confess that I probably deserved every moment of discipline I received.

When we think of discipline, that's usually the picture in our minds. Discipline always looks corrective. But discipline is not always corrective. Yes, it's true that it can be corrective, but not always. What we find in Scripture, and practically in our journey of faith, is that while discipline is not always corrective, it is always instructive. What I mean is that at all times and every season, God is instructing and guiding us in this journey. He's moving us along the path by his grace, and at times it's smooth sailing, and at other times we are just barely holding on. Discipline serves as the guardrails to our lives. They keep us on the right path, heading in the right direction. And God uses the difficult seasons to keep us on our intended target, Christlikeness.

Thankfully, this passage doesn't leave us empty-handed. It ends by giving us the motivation for godly discipline. The promise that the present discomfort will in the end yield fruit. Discipline now, endurance tomorrow, and eventually, fruit will come. By the way, this truth is seen practically in our world today. Consider any champion athlete. They didn't become a champion without discipline. Discipline is the difficult development that moves ability to mastery. Discipline is what has made Michael Jordan (or LeBron James depending on where you land in the argument) the GOAT (the Greatest Of All Time); Jack Nicklaus and Tiger Woods Major Champions; Serena Williams the greatest tennis player of all time; Wayne Gretzky the "Great One"; and Tom Brady a perennial MVP. Discipline is necessary to perfect a craft, ability, or skill. And when used correctly, it will produce victory in the right season. If this is true about discipline practically, how much more will it be spiritually? Valuable discipline in the present will lead to worthy fruit in the future.

While we know that discipline is an essential need for life, few of us would sign up for it voluntarily. That's the point of Hebrews 12. We are being called to act like people who are utterly persuaded that we have been adopted by faith and that our Omnipotent Father loves us so much that even the most painful adversities of our lives are expressions of his loving discipline and not his hateful vengeance. God is beckoning us to see his sometimes-painful work as expressions of loving discipline and to endure knowing that fruit will come in the future.

So, we know that God is ruling over the lives of his people. This means that the persecution, sickness, and adversity we endure are part of God's sovereign design for our good. How can we so be sure? Because it's God's grace that is at work to help us run this race of faith and ultimately to become more like Christ. To state it simply, grace is moving us along and discipline keeps us going in the right direction. I think we can all agree to the value of discipline in this way. But this is also where the work of grace can be misunderstood and consequently made an idol. Where do I get this? Well, after the author gives us this beautiful truth about discipline, he continues by describing its application:

> *Therefore lift your drooping hands and strengthen your weak knees, and make straight paths for your feet, so that what is lame may not be put out of joint but rather be healed. Strive*

for peace with everyone, and for the holiness without which no one will see the Lord. See to it that no one fails to obtain the grace of God; that no "root of bitterness" springs up and causes trouble, and by it many become defiled... (Hebrews 12:12–15)

The author transitions from speaking as a loving Father back to a track coach. But this time, the track coach has the whistle in his mouth. He gives command after command in order to get our attention. But there is one imperative that stands out as the controller of this section. In verse 15, he says to "See to it." This word literally means, "to look after, care for, or to oversee." It's like a boss watching over his employees. Or as I remind the team I work with, "Inspect what you expect." But what is it that we are supposed to inspect and expect? He says, "That no one fails to obtain the grace of God."

Pause here for a moment. Don't miss this. At first reading, it would seem that the writer is saying, "Hey, make sure you don't miss the grace of God and as a result lose it." We could naturally assume that he is warning us not to miss grace and somehow miss salvation. But I don't think that's what he's saying here. He was writing to Jewish believers who were facing immense persecution. Many of them were growing reluctant in their faith. Instead of running the race of faith, they were beginning to coast. They needed discipline. It's not that they needed more grace. No, instead they were missing out on what grace was able to do.

Now you might wonder, "Where do you get this idea?" Well, the words *fail to obtain* are actually one word. It's the Greek word *hustereo*, which means "to be left behind in a race, to lack, or to fall back." Let me paint the picture for you. A few summers ago, my family and I were out in the driveway shooting hoops. When I play basketball, especially against my four sons, I like to show a little bit of my old school b-ball skills. I like to think that I still can take them in whatever sport I play.

I played sports in high school and college. What I don't have in height, I make up for by being quick and scrappy (at least this used to be true). Anyway, we were in the driveway preparing for a little family game. Before the game started, one of my boys challenged me, "Dad, I don't think you can beat us in a race anymore." Well, those are the wrong words to say to this dad. So I responded, "Game on! I might be older, but I will humble you...embarrass you!" Of course, my wife, Allyson, was watching this and decided to stir things up a bit. "Dave, are you sure you want to do this? You're not as young as you used to be!"

If I'm being straightforward, I work better as an underdog. If it wasn't enough to have the challenge from my sons, now to have my wife challenge me. Invitation accepted! I will do whatever it takes to prove them wrong. So we headed up our driveway to race back down toward Mom. We lined up and Allyson called out the standard starting line orders, "On your mark... Get set... Go!" Now, let me tell you, I got a great start. As I was running, I felt like Rocky on the beach. I could imagine my muscles were bulging as I was punishing them with my speed. I started quickly and could tell I was going to win this race... easily. About two-thirds of the way through, I felt a breeze go by me as my two oldest boys blew by me at warp speed. It was as if I was just standing there. As I was nearing the finish line, I looked beside me and there was my youngest son getting ready to pass me. As if it wasn't bad enough to be beaten by my two oldest sons, I couldn't let my youngest beat me. So I gave him a little bump across the finish line.

Now at this point, I received exactly what I expected. My wife yelled out, "Well, they got you beat." My boys started talking smack.[1] So I did what any smart dad does. I looked at my family and I proudly said, "Guys, I wanted to encourage you by letting you finally win one." Just like the praise song says, I want to be a *Good, Good Father*. I smugly proclaimed, "I let you win." Don't miss this...that's exactly what this word, *hustereo*, means. We are all in a race of faith by grace. Grace is taking us on this journey, and we have a responsibility to keep up with where it's leading. The problem is, we aren't keeping up with where God desires to take us. Over and over again, we find ourselves falling behind, and so we come up with excuse after excuse. And when this happens, we can get easily frustrated and, slowly, bitterness can begin to set in. Grace becomes an idol.

---

1   Not sure where they got this from...I am positive their mom teaches them to do such things when I'm not around.

> **When grace becomes an idol, it becomes a source of bitterness instead of a place of breakthrough in your life.**

This is eye-opening. When we fall behind in our journey of faith, the grace that is supposed to motivate us in the race becomes a source of bitterness. The author describes this striking truth in verse 15, "See to it that no one fails to obtain the grace of God; that no 'root of bitterness' springs up and causes trouble, and by it many become defiled." Undoubtedly, grace is a wonderful thing, the greatest of all gifts ever given, but when you elevate it to a place it was never meant to be, separate it from God himself, it becomes the cause of great frustration. It becomes a burden. And grace that becomes an idol will eventually lead you to bitterness.

BITTERNESS OR BREAKTHROUGH

LET ME CONNECT THE DOTS for a moment. It is no surprise that verse 15 is actually a quote from the Old Testament. Approximately 70% of the book of Hebrews contains quotes from the Old Testament. This verse is actually a quote from Deuteronomy 29. In this chapter, Moses is standing before a new generation preparing to enter into the Promised Land. Over forty years have passed. The generation that came out of Egypt has passed away, except for two people, Joshua and Caleb. So Moses reminds them of the covenant that God made with the people forty years earlier when they exited Egypt. Notice the words that he declares to them,

> *You know how we lived in the land of Egypt, and how we came through the midst of the nations through which you passed. And you have seen their detestable things, their idols of wood and stone, of silver and gold, which were among them. Beware lest there be among you a man or woman or clan or tribe whose heart is turning away today from the Lord our God to go*

and serve the gods of those nations. Beware lest there be among
you a root bearing poisonous and bitter fruit, one who, when
he hears the words of this sworn covenant, blesses himself in his
heart, saying, "I shall be safe, though I walk in the stubbornness
of my heart." This will lead to the sweeping away of moist and
dry alike. (Deuteronomy 29:16–19)

He calls them to remember the generation that came out of
Egypt. What was supposed to be an eleven-day journey took them over
forty years. Why? Because they turned their hearts away from the grace
of God in the wilderness. Remember, God had acted graciously toward
them on multiple fronts. He graciously delivered them from the wick-
ed pharaoh of Egypt. He graciously delivered them through the im-
passable Red Sea. He graciously provided sustenance in the wilderness
on multiple occasions through manna and water. All of the gracious
acts of God afforded them in the wilderness wanderings should have
only intensified their endurance.

Knowing God had been gracious over and over again should
have caused them to hold on to the hope of the Promised Land all the
more. But along the way, they grew ungrateful. They began to coast. They
began to lag behind. And slowly, these amazingly gracious acts watered a
root of bitterness in them. It caused them to say, "If God could do those
things for us, why can't he just deliver us into the Promised Land now?"
It's like a child in the back seat, "Are we there yet?" I wonder if this statement actually began in the wilderness. "If God is so gracious, why are we
taking so long to get to this land that has been promised?"

You could probably hear the bitterness growing. And eventually the root begins to sprout. Notice the wording in Deuteronomy 29:
the "root of bitterness" became "poison" to them. The wording here is
very powerful. In fact, most scholars would agree that this bitter herb
was most likely gall. Gall is one of the most bitter plants in biblical
times. Many compare it to poppy. Most interesting is its use. When it
was mixed with wine, it would take the edge off of people who were
dying and at the same time quicken the dying process because it would
poison the person from the inside out. In fact, the Romans used it in

the first century during crucifixions. Whatever the substance, Moses reminds them that the grace that should have caused them to break through in the wilderness began to grow bitterness in them. Bitterness that can overflow life like a poisonous parasite.

I don't know if you have ever had a parasite or not. I have, and I will never forget its effect. Early in my ministry, I served as young adult and singles pastor at a church in the Washington, DC, area. One of our missionaries served with New Tribes Missions in a remote village in Papua New Guinea. Wanting to immerse young adults into deep mission experiences, we decided to go on a trip to visit these missionaries and do some work at a mission base in a larger city of Papua New Guinea. Midway through our trip, a few of us flew into the jungle to visit with our missionaries serving this remote tribe. I have to confess, it would still be considered one of the highlights of my spiritual life. Meeting people who had never heard the name of Jesus and realizing that we were only a few of the people in the world who would ever see this tribe was both exhilarating and life changing.

While visiting the missionaries in the jungle, we were invited to join the tribal chief and some tribal leaders for dinner. Their tribal specialty was on the menu…baked potatoes. Not just any baked potatoes, but potatoes cooked in the ash of a fire in the center of their hut. The potatoes were good, the company was amazing. But it was this moment that changed the experience entirely. The next morning, I grew immensely sick. And not to overstate the point, but I was sicker than I had ever been. I couldn't keep anything down. I began to lose weight. In fact, I barely could make it home. When I did get home, I immediately went to the doctor, where they confirmed what we had expected: I had a parasite…a dreaded, potentially deadly, parasite. In fact, it was so bad that I had to take medicine given to cancer patients. It was the nastiest thing I have ever experienced.

When I read Deuteronomy 29, I get it. What begins as a beautifully provided meal, God's grace, becomes a root of bitterness. We look at life and begin to say, "God, you're gracious, but you're not providing what I need." Slowly we stop seeing the power and majesty of God's grace at work in our lives, and we begin to say, "God, you are short-changing me. You are holding back from me. You are not providing for me in the way that you should (whether it's spiritually, physically, emotionally, or mentally). In some ways, you are failing me, God!" And what happens? It becomes a root of bitterness, and then eventually the parasite takes over.

And notice the text tells us that this poison does two things: it "causes troubles" and "defiles many." What does this mean? Well, bitterness is like an acid that destroys its own container. It will eat you from the inside out. And when your heart grows bitter, God will seem distant to you. And if we no longer enjoy all that God has done for us, we begin to idol-chase. Instead of God's grace breaking us through the difficulty of life, bitterness destroys our perspective and leads to more and more trouble. Have you ever noticed how trouble seems to follow trouble? That's the picture. The root of bitterness that results at what we perceive to be trouble only grows into more trouble.

But the cycle of bitterness doesn't stop there. It doesn't just stop at us. Notice it says that this poison eventually "defiles many." The poison is highly contagious. Like a poisonous weed, it infiltrates the rest of the garden. Isn't this so true? We see this all the time in the relationships of our families, places of employment, and even the world of Christianity. This fruit of sin quickly becomes social and shows itself in various forms. It can come in forms of jealousy, envy, coldness, resentment, unforgiveness, apathy, avoidance, withdrawal, gossip, slander, and even criticism.

All of these stem from a failure to understand how God is leading us by his grace to precisely where he desires us to be in this journey of faith. If we just keep running, grace will break us through in his timing. No, instead, we begin to take things in our own hands. By the way, the root of bitterness is underground; it is easy to hide and camouflage. Seldom do you find anyone who will admit that they are a bitter person. Haven't you found that to be true to life? Bitter people never admit they are bitter. It's a deep and unseen way of life. And like any parasite, what is in you will sooner or later come out of you. And in this journey it won't just affect us; it will deeply impact those around us as well. We probably have all seen this. Bitterness leads to sour relationships, doesn't it? Bitter people hurt people. We do well to look at our lives and ask, "Has a root of bitterness set in?"

THE POWER TO FINISH

WHEN GRACE SUBTLY BECOMES AN idol, we stop racing and we start coasting. Bitterness sets in…toward God and life. So how do we respond? How can we have staying power and not an easy exit mentality? How can we be confident that we can finish this journey well? There are three things to consider and practice: (1) Grace provides us with a proper perspective of the journey, (2) Grace actively moves us in the right direction, (3) Grace will never leave us unfulfilled.

GRACE PROVIDES A PROPER PERSPECTIVE OF THE JOURNEY

GRACE GIVES US A PROPER perspective of the journey. Why? Because it's God's grace. God, at times a coach and at times a father, knows exactly where he is leading us. Now I know that sounds cliché, but God uses grace as the precise instrument that keeps us moving in the right direction. And we can be especially assured that we are ultimately being led to Christlikeness and holiness. Therefore, we can have a proper perspective about anything that happens in life. How can this be true? Because we have God's grace. Notice Hebrews 12:12 says, "Therefore lift your drooping hands and strengthen your weak knees, and make straight paths for your feet, so that what is lame may not be put out of joint but rather be healed." It's no accident that the track language continues.

I don't know if you have ever run a marathon. I certainly haven't. I've run a few 5ks, but I consider people who run 26.2 miles to be a little crazy. I mean, if there were doughnuts along the way, I might be in. Otherwise, I find it to be a good waste of distance, especially considering I can jump in the car and drive twenty-six miles in a short time. Now, I do know a few marathoners. Whenever I meet someone who has run a marathon, I'm always intrigued by their journey. What's funny is that almost all of them describe a similar experience. Somewhere around miles 19–21 they hit a crucial moment that they call "the wall." At this key moment, they are absolutely exhausted and everything in them is ready to quit. Mentally they are fried. Their mouth grows dry. Their legs become heavy as they begin to cramp. Their feet are blistered. And their bodies are yelling, "Give up!" They describe this mental moment where you have to talk yourself into finishing. It's the moment of breakthrough to finish the marathon.

That's exactly what verse 12 is describing. Grace gives us the spiritual capacity to lift the arms that are drooping from exhaustion. It causes us to strengthen our knees. By the way, this is an interesting Greek word for *strengthen our knees*. It's where we get our word *orthopedic*. It literally means "to set or straighten the bone." Clearly, the author is not talking about a knee replacement. His point is that grace should spiritually reinforce us for the race. Grace, when properly understood, gives us the capacity in our weakest moments of the race to keep going…to finish. It's like the coach yelling in our most exhausted moment, "Don't give up! Don't give in! Suck it up! You can finish!" Except in our spiritual journey it's so much stronger, because it's not a "suck it up, grin and bear it" mentality. In Christianity we have something that is strong enough to draw our focus away from the temporary pain and lead us into an eternal purpose: grace. It gives us the proper perspective to not quit. It's the picture of a runner who is both fighting through the fatigue and being refreshed by grace. And because we know that what grace starts it finishes, we can keep our mind on the ultimate prize.

GRACE ACTIVELY MOVES US IN THE RIGHT DIRECTION

NOT ONLY DOES IT GIVE us a right perspective, it also moves us in the right direction. This is why endurance is so important. Endurance has two aspects. It's not only an established purpose but also an intended target. The worst thing that can happen in any race is to take a wrong turn. How does grace keep us moving in the right direction? Well, Hebrews 12:14 continues, "Strive for peace with everyone, and for the holiness without which no one will see the Lord." The author describes two things here. He says, "Strive for peace with everyone," and "strive for holiness." Notice the race extends to both our relationship with others and also our relationship with God. Peace with others and holiness for God. These are both driven by the action "to strive." Again, another word that paints a powerful picture is διώκω, *diókó*, which means "to hunt aggressively." It's the idea of chasing an enemy until you have completely destroyed them. This is a Jason Bourne moment. Except it's not to take them out (although there might be times we feel that way) but to make peace. Grace calls us to aggressively pursue peace with other people who are in our journey.

Notice it doesn't say that we will be at peace with all people. Even Jesus himself said, "The world will hate you because they hated me." This is certainly true around the world. We can also see a rising attitude of criticism toward Christianity in our own culture. Some of it is rightly so, some of it is our own fault, but some of it is because the Scripture tells us that this will be a reality. In fact, as Christians we can't escape it. Consequently, we are not going to be at peace with every person. But we are reminded to pursue peace aggressively with everyone we can. How do we do that? By grace. In the context, peace is an outcome of the Father's discipline. So, when I know that God is at work through the difficulties of life, even when I'm wounded or hurt, I can live and respond with peace. Grace allows me to make room for peace in every relationship whatever the cost and whenever the time.

Let's continue the track analogy for a moment. If you ever watched a long-distance race, I am certain you have seen the pictures of exhausted runners helping other weaker runners cross the finish line at the end of the race. Why? Because it's not just about finishing the race first, it's about finishing the race well. This is equally true in our Christian journeys. The reason we pursue peace with others is because we realize that they are on this difficult journey as well. Maybe not at the same place we are, but nonetheless, we are in it together. The more we understand this, the more that the pursuit of peace makes sense. Who are the people in your life that necessitate an aggressive pursuit of peace? Are you running after peace? If not, you will fall behind in the race of faith, and bitterness will begin to set in.

Grace also moves us into a quest for holiness. Please don't miss that peace is described as a two-way street. Our relationship with others doesn't trump our relationship with God. It affects others as it is directly connected to God. In fact, I would dare say that our pursuit of peace becomes more effective when we are also pursuing holiness.

I have found in my own Christian life that the natural outworking of pursuing Christlikeness is that I also end up being more peaceful in the way I live and react to others. Of course, there are also cases in which a stand for holiness can result in a loss of peace. When our stand for holiness runs against the grain of the world, peace might be difficult. In those cases, we should strive for peace but not at the expense of holiness. Peace can rule in us even when there is chaos around us. Whatever the situation, it's important to recognize that a pursuit of holiness is not a race to perfection. Certainly, on this side of eternity, that is not going to happen. Instead, chasing after holiness is ultimately submitting to where God is leading me in life. To live with the end, Christlikeness, in view.

This means that I have to look at the small, intimate places in my spiritual life where I am lacking, slowing, or struggling and where God is beckoning me to be holy. I love how Charles Spurgeon described this, "You will never gain holiness by standing still. Nobody ever grew holy without agonizing to be holy. Sin will grow without sowing, but holiness needs cultivation. Follow it—it will not run after you. You must pursue it with determination, with eagerness, with perseverance as a hunter pursues its prey."[2] He is saying that we have a responsibility to run after holiness. While we know that God will one day make every Christian holy, on this side of eternity, God doesn't force this pursuit on us. He leaves it to our striving. This begins by identifying the areas that might be slowing us down, the roadblocks that can potentially be tripping us up.

It's like driving. As my sons began to practice driving, I would say to them, "You need to constantly be on the lookout for what's ahead and react appropriately. If a car is making a turn, you have to see it first. If an animal is lurking along the side of a back road, you have to be ready. If the light up ahead turns yellow, it doesn't mean

2   Ernest LeVos, *Portraits of the Great "I Am": Charles Spurgeon on Christ's Seven "I Am" Sayings* (Bloomington, IN: iUniverse, 2017), 180.

you speed up; it means you begin to slow down."[3] Driving well means you are looking at the roadblocks that might be ahead and dealing appropriately in that moment.

In the same way, the warning signs and roadblocks that will take us off course spiritually have far greater implications. And we do well to pay attention to them. Consequently, desiring a holy life does not mean that we detest one area of sin and put up with another. It's a call to cleanse our lives, to hunt down the areas of sinfulness that can slow up our race and get rid of them. It would be like saying, "Oh, I have an anger problem," and accept that this is just the way I am. We have to identify these sinful tendencies and lay them aside along with the excuses that accompany them. Then, and only then, can we willingly strive for holiness.

Grace, properly applied, keeps us in the right direction. It moves us toward peace with others and holiness for God. It's like MapQuest giving us directions toward the finish line of godliness. But when grace is an idol, it becomes like a game of pin the tail on the donkey. If we get it right, we got lucky. And the misses will only lead to more frustration and bitterness. Our role is to pursue grace's direction. At times the pursuit will be uncomfortable, even painful. But we have to submit to the grace-filled encouragement of a coach who has experienced the race, Jesus, and the grace-filled discipline of a loving father who knows the right way.

GRACE WILL NEVER LEAVE US UNFULFILLED

GRACE WILL NEVER LEAVE US unfulfilled...ultimately. It might not happen in our timing or in the way we think it should, but if we trust the work of God's grace, it will never leave us unfulfilled. When we attempt to speed up the journey or attempt to manipulate it our way, we make grace an idol. The author of Hebrews makes this exact point with an analogy at the end of this passage.

> *That no one is sexually immoral or unholy like Esau, who sold his birthright for a single meal. For you know that afterward,*

---

3   Confession...I am guilty of this. I bet I'm not the only one?

when he desired to inherit the blessing, he was rejected, for
he found no chance to repent, though he sought it with tears.
(Hebrews 12:16–17)

The story of the twins Jacob and Esau is one of the most intriguing in the Old Testament. Abraham had the son of promise, Isaac. Isaac then becomes the proud father of twins, Esau the elder and Jacob the younger. As was the culture in that day, their names were given in relation to their appearance or character. Esau means "hairy" and later in the story he becomes Edom for "red hair." Jacob appropriately means "grabber of the heel" due to the fact that he was most likely holding Esau's heel at birth. Jacob can also mean "deceiver," potentially giving insight into his deceptive nature throughout his story in Genesis. As the oldest, Esau had the full birthright privileges and the greatest access to the future inheritance. And that is where we see the plot twist.

Once when Jacob was cooking stew, Esau came in from the
field, and he was exhausted. And Esau said to Jacob, "Let me
eat some of that red stew, for I am exhausted!" (Therefore his
name was called Edom.) Jacob said, "Sell me your birthright
now." Esau said, "I am about to die; of what use is a birthright
to me?" Jacob said, "Swear to me now." So he swore to him and
sold his birthright to Jacob. Then Jacob gave Esau bread and
lentil stew, and he ate and drank and rose and went his way.
Thus Esau despised his birthright. (Genesis 25:29–34)

Now don't miss this image. Esau shows up after a long day of hunting, preparing the kill, and providing for the family. He's exhausted and hungry. He comes home and his brother, Jacob, is cooking some beef stew. And it must have smelled really good and looked scrumptious. So Jacob offers his famished brother a deal, his birthright for some stew. Now when I read this story, I can't help but ask, what in the world was Esau thinking? Well, the simple answer is he didn't need the birthright at that precise moment. He says as much. If he is dead, a birthright won't do him any good. It has no use at this point in his journey. There was a long waiting period until the birthright would be fully realized. And so he gives it away for a bowl of soup. Sustenance became more important than inheritance.

So what point is the author of Hebrews attempting to tell us about grace? Here's the point. We have been given God's grace at salvation. And that grace has lavishly granted us God's continuing work in our lives today. But then life doesn't happen the way that we think. Our spiritual journey takes a turn that we don't expect. In those crucible moments, how easy is it for us to take the grace of God and trade it for a proverbial bowl of soup? How many times do we take the birthright of grace, the guarantee of our future, and take something cheaper? We mistakenly think, "Life is short, and I need to make the most of it any way that I can." Ironically, the satisfaction is only temporary. And eventually, it will only lead us to a bitter tasting experience. We do well to watch out for the Esau Syndrome: trading away God's lifelong gift in order to satisfy a short-term appetite.

What's your appetite? What do you hunger for? Is it more grace? Is it a deeper understanding of grace? You know what I have found true in my life? Your greatest appetites will always drive your most significant decisions. What do you look at in your life and say, "If I just had this I'd be satisfied"? If grace is not fulfilling us, satisfying our deepest longings, then we have made it an idol. And the hunger to get will become greater than the desire to be. Let me encourage you—don't cheapen the birthright that God's grace has given you. Don't trade it for anything this world offers. Or to state it a different way, don't seek horizontally what has been fully supplied vertically by grace. Let God's grace lead you in this race, and breakthroughs will happen.

During the summer of my senior year of high school, I took a trip to South Africa. While there, we had the privilege of spending a couple of nights at Kruger National Park. It's one of the largest open game reserves in Africa at about 7,500 square miles. To put that in perspective, it's roughly the size of the state of New Jersey. This beautiful park is filled with thousands of amazing animals. One of the most abundant and beautiful animals to see in the park is the African impala. Now, please don't compare this animal with the likeness of the Chevy Impala. This comparison fails in many ways. The car cannot match the majesty of the animal.[4]

This quickly became one of my favorite animals because of its impressive ability to jump. The impala can jump 10 feet in the air for a distance of 30 feet. This means it can almost jump the entire length of a bus. But what makes this animal even more interesting is that you can build a 3 feet concrete wall around it and it will not jump. Why? Because it won't jump where it cannot see its feet land. You know, similarly, I believe many people are like the African impala when it comes to their journey of faith. God calls us to trust him along the journey. His grace gives us the freedom to enjoy all that he offers. But the world puts a wall around us. It causes us to feel trapped. And unfortunately, we begin to blame God for it. As a result, bitterness begins to take route in our lives instead of realizing the amazing freedom that lies on the other side of grace-based living—a life of peace and holiness.

When we begin to take the reins of grace, bitterness will set in and tell you the lie that God has failed you, short-changed you, and that you need to seek something else. And you know what ends up happening? The grace that is meant to instruct us will deprive us. The grace that is meant to discipline us will seem like a disadvantage. And the one thing considered the greatest gift of all, grace, will become a burden. May we not trade the grace of God for any cheap imitation but run the race in the abundance of grace. God may take us where we would never intend to go, but he will do it to produce in us what we could never achieve on our own. Breakthrough or bitterness? It's yours to choose.

---

4   Sorry not sorry Chevy lovers.

NOW WHAT?

Read: Hebrews 11-12; Deuteronomy 29

Discuss:

1. The writer of Hebrews uses a racing analogy to discuss our journey of faith (Hebrews 12:1-2). In what ways is this analogy appropriate for our Christian walk? How is this race analogy shown through the phrase "see to it that no one fails to obtain the grace of God" (Hebrews 12:15)? What does it look to fall behind in God's gracious work?

2. How does the idol version of grace cause bitterness in our lives? What trouble have you seen as a result of distorted grace? How has it affected others around you?

3. The writer of Hebrews describes how grace drives us toward peace and holiness. The word "strives" means to aggressively pursue. What does it look like to strive for peace and holiness? How do these two concepts work together? What makes them so difficult? Might there be cases in which a stand for holiness might result in a loss of peace?

4. Describe the example of Esau in Hebrews 12:16: How do we trade the grace of God for "soup" (cheap imitations)? How is grace our "birthright"? In what ways does biblical grace remind us that the desire to "be" must be greater than the hunger to "do"?

Pray:

Pray that your appetite for God's grace in your life will be greater than any other appetite the world has to offer

Memorize/Meditate:

"See to it that no one fails to obtain the grace of God; that no "root of bitterness" springs up and causes trouble, and by it many become defiled" (Hebrews 12:15).

COMMON GRACE

...set your hope fully on the grace that will be brought to you at the revelation of Jesus Christ. (1 Peter 1:13)

YEARS AGO, SOME FRIENDS WHO attended a young married group my wife and I led at our church in the Washington, DC, suburbs invited us to join them on a visit to their hometown in California. We had never been to California and were looking forward to a week of sightseeing, shopping, and, most importantly, time with our friends. They lived about two and a half hours from San Francisco. Ironically enough, one of my dreams was to visit Alcatraz, better known as the Rock. I know that sounds weird, but I had written a paper on the history of Alcatraz in high school and had been captivated by its story ever since. Criminals like Al Capone, Robert Franklin Stroud (the "Birdman of Alcatraz"), and George "Machine Gun" Kelly were some of the notorious criminals that were housed there. Add to that the attempted escapes. I loved the intrigue surrounding the place. Since our friends lived so close, they were gracious enough to take us.

On our once-in-a-lifetime tour, one thing that struck me most about the prison was the way it was built to hide the beauty of San Francisco Bay and the city. If you walked the perimeter of the island, it was stunningly beautiful, but once you entered the prison compound, the view disappeared. It was this small, yet intentional, fact that plagued the minds of many inmates. When they brought inmates to the island, before they entered behind the walls, they wanted them to fully experience the views of one of the most beautiful cities in the US. In reality, this was meant to play mind games with the prisoners.

Our tour guide explained to us that it was this exact thing that made Alcatraz such a hard place to serve time. The knowledge that just outside of the prison walls was one of the best views on the planet caused some of the inmates to literally go insane. For decades, criminals came and went; yet few, if any, experienced the beauty that was just outside the gates. Our tour guide described this as a great dichotomy of Alcatraz. Why? Because the inmates would have done anything to experience the freedom, to enjoy the beauty outside the prison, while less than a mile away, many of the residents of San Francisco just wanted to escape the city. They were accustomed to its beauty. For them it was everyday, normal, and routine. The mindset of "been there, done that" was the mantra for many who resided in the city.

WHEN GRACE BECOMES COMMON

How MANY OF US HAVE this same experience with the beauty of grace? God graciously gives us freedom from the bondage of sin. It's grace that is beyond human description. But God continues to pour upon our salvation gifts like Scripture, prayer, the church, our families, friends, jobs, and possessions. And these are just a few of the many we could count. But over time, what happens to each of these grace-filled gifts? Over and over again, we take them for ourselves and slowly begin to live as if they are merely common. No longer are they experienced with the splendor intended by their Giver. Instead, they become a normal, ho-hum, lackluster part of our lives.

There are many Scripture passages that illustrate this point well. But none more than what we read in 2 Samuel 6. It's the story about Uzzah's death when he touched the ark of the covenant. Whenever I read this passage, it stops me in my tracks. It's a story that if you were reading for the first time, you think you know where it's going but then shock and awe comes over you. The unexpected happens. It leaves me scratching my head, asking, "What in the world was God thinking?"

Second Samuel 6 begins as an amazing period in Israel's history. In fact, this could be considered an immensely important transitional moment. Israel's first king, Saul, had died at the hand of the Philistines. And David, who had already been anointed, was now crowned the new king of Israel. The first thing that David sought to do as king was defeat the Philistines. God led Israel to a decisive victory by the hand of David (2 Samuel 5). Now what happens next explains clearly what made David different than any other leader but also demonstrates what is possibly David's greatest, yet most understated, lesson. See, David doesn't just lead Israel to destroy the enemy; he also realizes there was something of tremendous value missing from Jerusalem...the ark of the covenant. It wasn't enough for David to have the geographic center of the nation free from enemy influence; he also realized the need to have the representation of God's presence in Jerusalem. This meant that David was committed, no matter the cost, to bring the ark back to God's people.

Now the obvious question is, "Why?" What was so important about an old gold box? It's actually true that the *ark* was merely a box. In fact, the word ark means "chest or box." It was a forty-five inch by twenty-seven-inch box made of acacia wood. It was overlaid in pure gold and topped by a golden grate they called the mercy seat. On either side of the mercy seat were two golden cherubim. No big deal, right?

Well, inside were three important items that reminded Israel of their historical significance and God's faithfulness through the years. Inside was the second copy of the Ten Commandments, written by the hand of God (remember Moses destroyed the first copy); a golden pot filled with manna to remind the people of God's provision in the wilderness;[1] and Aaron's rod that budded flowers to remind the people of God's choice of the tribe of Levi as the priestly tribe. But the ark was more than a mere historical box. It was also the most significant physical representation of God's presence, holiness, and grace. Exodus 25:22 says that it was between the two cherubim on the mercy seat that God would meet with the people of Israel and give them direction and commandments.

In essence, the ark represented God's word to God's people. God led the Hebrews through the ark. As a result, there were clear in-

---

1   I always love when people ask what manna is...because "manna" actually means "What is it?" in Hebrew. Your guess is as good as mine. Although oatmeal cream pies would be my guess.

structions about how to treat the ark. It wasn't to be touched or looked upon, and was to be carried in a precise way. The high priest was the only person allowed to see the ark and, even then, only once per year on the Day of Atonement (or Yom Kippur). When they moved the ark, they were instructed to collapse the Tabernacle over it and carry it with specially designed poles. As you can imagine, this process was pretty meticulous. It only enhanced the holy significance of the ark to the people of God. Ironically, even Hollywood gets this perspective correct in movies pertaining to the ark. Remember the classic *Indiana Jones and the Raiders of the Lost Ark*. When the Nazis looked inside the ark, their flesh melted.

So what happened to the ark that caused David to desire its return to Jerusalem? We are told in 1 Samuel 5–6, some seventy-five years earlier, that Eli's evil sons began to use the ark of the covenant as a type of good-luck charm or rabbit's foot. They would pull it out during times of battle and believed that it would assure victory. The problem was, God was having none of it. Eventually, the Philistines captured it. But it didn't go well for the Philistines either. God punished them the entire time the ark was in their possession.

So they took the ark back to Israel's land and left it at the house of a man named Abinadab. For twenty years, it sat on his property. Saul didn't bother with it. But David, with all spiritual sensitivity, believed it was the way Israel could best return to God. Now seventy-five years later, David is about to bring the ark back to Jerusalem. And this is precisely where the story goes south. Second Samuel describes the scene. Basically, they throw a military parade. There is great fanfare…a marching band and a crazy celebration. You could imagine the excitement that was being shared in Jerusalem, "God is coming home, baby!"

However, one pertinent note stands out. "And they carried the ark of God on a *new cart* and brought it out of the house of Abinadab, which was on the hill. And Uzzah and Ahio, the sons of Abinadab, were driving the new cart" (2 Samuel 6:3, emphasis added). And this is when the unexpected happened. "And when they came to the threshing floor of Nacon, Uzzah put out his hand to the ark of God and took hold of it, for the oxen stumbled. And the anger of the Lord was kindled against Uzzah, and God struck him down there because of his error, and he died there beside the ark of God" (2 Samuel 6:6–7).

I have to confess, we could produce an entire book from this passage alone. There are so many small, yet peculiar details that make this story so intriguing. For example, the oxen stumble on the threshing floor. The threshing floor would have been the most level and smoothest portion of the journey to Jerusalem.[2] But that's an insignificant detail when you consider what happened to Uzzah. To say it doesn't seem fair would be an understatement. This not only isn't fair; it doesn't make sense. It would certainly seem that Uzzah was doing God a favor. I mean, come on—he was protecting the ark from falling off the cart. His intentions were certainly faultless.

Here's a small side note we should consider—good intentions cannot be equated with a proper approach to God. The best intentions in the world don't necessarily mean that I am making the proper approach to the things of God. Sincere intentions can still be sincerely wrong. This story is probably more about approach than we realize. Now please know, this is not to say that intentions are worthless. But good intentions alone don't necessarily produce a godly impact. We all know people who have great intentions but aren't living out God's will.

David's reaction gives us all that we need to know concerning why he believed God did this. Second Samuel 6 tells us that David takes three months to ponder this mistake.[3] You can't help but imagine what was going through their minds during this time. The text tells us that David moves from anger *toward* God to fear *of* God. No doubt, anger would appear to be a proper human response in this moment. But anger is quickly overtaken by the more appropriate response of fear. Why is fear more appropriate? While anger can certainly be a proper feel-

---

2   The threshing floor would be positioned at the top of a hill. This would allow the breeze to blow away the chaff so that the grain could be more easily gathered from the floor.

3   Another ironic moment…throughout the ninety days, they leave the ark at the house of Obed-Edom the Gittite. This time must have been so overwhelming they don't leave it with an Israelite; they leave it with a pagan Gittite.

ing in certain situations, it usually doesn't lead to a proper response. Where can anger go? Unless it's humbly set aside or filtered through wisdom, anger usually is followed by regrettable consequences.

But fear can be an immensely valuable gift when used correctly. The Scripture shows this over and over again. In fact, fear shows up over three hundred times in the Scripture. And if you could divide each of the passages that reference fear, you would find that fear toward circumstances or people is usually misplaced, and fear toward God is almost always appropriate. Because fear toward the right person or object can lead to healthy, valuable responses. For three months David pondered how he should respond to this deep fear he was experiencing.

So what did David conclude? We find the answer in 1 Chronicles 15, the correlating passage to 2 Samuel 6. David says, "Because you did not carry it the first time, the Lord our God broke out against us, because we did not seek him according to the rule" (1 Chronicles 15:13). David realized that they did not follow the prescribed plan of God for moving the ark. Instead of carrying the ark as God had commanded, they just put it on a "new cart." The implication is that they copied the Philistine plan to move the ark. They simply changed the cart.

Three months later, they do it over. And the posture is completely different. Instead of carrying the ark on a cart, they carry it with poles as originally commanded. By the way, can you imagine the pole bearers being called in for the task? I imagine a few of them called in sick, especially considering what happened with Uzzah. But the careful nature of this moment goes to another level, as it describes that they sacrificed an ox and another fatted animal after six steps.[4] Now, I don't know if you have ever sacrificed an ox as a burnt offering. I have burned a couple of burgers on the grill—that certainly takes some time. But can you imagine burning an ox to ash? This would be neither quick nor easy.

The enormity of this moment is only enhanced by what happens next. It says that David danced before the Lord in a linen ephod.

---

4   Some scholars believe that they actually sacrificed every six steps back to Jerusalem. First Chronicles 15 says they sacrificed seven bulls and seven rams. Whether it was once, seven times, or every six steps, the intensity of this moment doesn't change.

Why is this noteworthy? Because the first time they attempted to move the ark, David was dressed in royal clothing as an acknowledgement of his military victories. But with this second attempt, he wore the undergarments of the common priest. Why? Because the focus of this journey wasn't Israel's victory, but God himself. If you want to grasp the beauty of this moment, read Psalm 24. Many scholars believe this psalm was sung as the ark was being brought into the city of Jerusalem. The well-known refrain is "Who is the King of Glory?" That describes wonderfully the focus of this second attempt.

Now, I know the question you are probably asking, "What in the world does this have to do with grace?" Well, the answer is found in the exact reason the second attempt to move the ark was so different than the first. It's much more significant than whether the ark was carried or not. It's deeper than whether they should have sacrificed after six steps or David wore the garments of the priest. The passage serves as a reminder and warning that we must be careful to not allow holy things to become common things. And this is exactly how grace becomes an idol in the first place.

> **Grace becomes an idol when we cease to acknowledge it as holy.**

Grace can take the same journey as the ark of the covenant. Instead of being a gift that serves as a holy reflection of God himself, it becomes a gift we use to get what we think we need in our lives. Grace can become a rallying cry, rabbit's foot, and routine all at the same time. When disconnected from its connection to God, it can become normal, lackluster, and common. It becomes a mere artifact in our lives instead of the active pursuit of our lives. That is exactly what happened to the ark of the covenant. As a result, we do well to continually remember that grace is Divine, holy.

WHERE GRACE AND HOLINESS MEET

THE STORY IN 2 SAMUEL 6 gives us a flawless case study in the holiness of God. No doubt, there are entire volumes written on the topic of holiness. Now, I realize that we touched on the topic of holiness in the last chapter, but only as it relates to our character in the journey that grace is leading us on. Here, we do well to connect holiness to grace as it relates uniquely to the character of God.

In our culture today, I would argue that holiness gets a bad rap. We describe people as "holier than thou" as if they were some kind of moral nerd. In many ways, the idea of holiness has become more of a vice than virtue. Unfortunately, holiness has lost…well…its holiness. By definition, the word *holy* is extremely expressive throughout the Scripture. Both the Hebrew Old Testament word (*qadosh*) and the Greek New Testament word (*hagios*) carry the same weight in their meanings. Holiness can be defined as "to be separate, set apart, unique, uncommon, or in a category of its own." Whatever object is connected to holiness is elevated out of the sphere of the ordinary. As it relates to God, holiness is the quality that describes his absolute purity, glory, and power. So when we are referring to God's grace, it takes a whole new depth of understanding and effect.

Grace and holiness are uniquely intertwined all throughout the Scripture. Much like grace and truth, grace and holiness seem to provide a necessary balance to the Christian journey. They motivate and protect each other from losing effectiveness in our lives. Second Samuel 6 gives us a good picture of this balance, as it shows us David and Israel basking in the grace of God (upon leading them to victory) while at the same time reminding them that holiness matters.

I believe we find ourselves in a similar hinge-point in modern Christianity. While we see a strong movement centered on the concept of grace, there seems to be a growing weakness and hesitation when it comes to the area of holiness. We almost treat them as competing forces tugging against each other instead of enhancing each other. If you listen to conversations about grace, you almost sense a fear to approach the topic of holiness. Because…how could holiness be gracious?

The opposite is also true. It's as if a gracious God is extremely kind and a holy God is unexplainably mean. So why would anyone want to touch holiness at the expense of grace? The hesitation to connect the two has created a sense of superficiality in our approach to God's grace. Coincidently, we brand the word *grace* without a full understanding of what it means, and as a result we develop popular misconceptions as it relates to our lives. The problem is, you can't have true, life-altering grace without a holy, amazing God. God is what makes grace so amazing. That's what this book has been about. Any separation of holiness and grace make it more about grace than God.

A PROPER VIEW OF GRACE

So how do we approach grace with holiness in mind, and how does holiness act as an antidote to an idol form of grace? Peter, the apostle and first leader of the church, gives us the answer in 1 Peter 1. Of all the apostles, Peter understood the holy position of grace in a unique way as both the disciple who denied Christ and the one who was restored by Christ. So he encourages the church, "Therefore, preparing your minds for action, and being sober-minded, set your hope fully on the grace that will be brought to you at the revelation of Jesus Christ" (1 Peter 1:13). A proper view of grace begins with our thinking.

HAVE THE RIGHT MINDSET

If the goal is to battle grace from becoming overfamiliar and taking an idol form, it begins with proper thinking about what grace is actually doing in our lives. Peter encourages believers to set their minds fully on the grace that is yet to come to us at the coming of Jesus. That means grace's work is still not yet fully complete. While at the same time, our minds and hope can be fully set on grace's work only as it is connected to Christ and his work. In other words, it's not a grab and go mentality. There is a constant need to have right thinking about what grace is accomplishing in our lives and where it is spiritually taking us.

This is the centrality of the gospel message. The gospel isn't just that Christ came to earth, died on a cross, and rose again and now offers salvation through his grace. If that is all it is, it's an incomplete gospel. The gospel also includes the fact that work being done through grace is not yet complete but promises to be through death or the second coming of Jesus Christ. The gospel is all three: the death, resurrection, and the second coming of Jesus Christ. This must be at the forefront of our thinking as it relates to grace. This is grace in its holy form and function. Otherwise, grace will be easily manipulated and twisted.

I love the words Peter uses to describe this type of thinking. In essence, he says the same thing three different ways, "Prepare your minds, be sober-minded, and set your hope fully." The term *prepare your minds for action* is literally "gird up your loins." Now probably none of us use this type of language anymore. We don't look at our kids and say, "Gird up your loins, we are going out to the ballgame." If we did, we would quickly become a meme that gets a lot of laughs. But the idea of this phrase paints a fantastic picture of the right thinking we need to have about grace. In biblical times when you would "gird up your loins," you lifted up your robe so you could run. Some even wore a sash that would act as a holder for the robe so they could run unhindered.

This reminds me of a Cleveland Indians game I attended recently. Sometime in the middle of the game, they usually have a few mascots race around the field. In Cleveland they have multiple mascots dressed like famous condiments…ketchup, mustard, and relish. These characters are chosen as fun mascots because of a famous stadium mustard found at Cleveland sporting events. Whether the mustard is actually good or not is highly debatable. Nonetheless, at Indians games, they bring a little bit of fun and a family feel by having these mascots race each other or chase a hotdog character.

During one particular race, the hotdog character was having a hard time running because the costume limited the mobility of his or her legs, much like running in a skirt. As the character made its way around the field, it tripped and face-planted right in front of the home-plate umpire, who without hesitation, called it out. As you can imagine, it created widespread laughter across the stadium. Needless to say, the hotdog mascot needed to "gird up his loins." Without right thinking about grace's work, we will fall flat on our spiritual faces and grace will become to us what God never intended. It will be misaligned and misapplied, leaving us with more confusion than confidence.

In fact, what Peter says next makes this point all the more obvious. When it comes to grace, I must constantly think about what grace is doing and where grace is taking me. Simply put, if it's disconnected from God and his work in my life, it's probably going to lead me in a faulty direction. We need to ask questions like how is grace amplifying the gospel's sanctifying movement in my life? Is there an area where I am manipulating God's grace to get my way? Is there an area I am misapplying grace as God intended? The point is that I must constantly set my mind on the gospel work of grace.

Peter takes this one step further. "As obedient children, do not be conformed to the passions of your former ignorance, but as he who called you is holy, you also be holy in all your conduct" (1 Peter 1:14–15). It's not enough for us to merely have a proper thinking about grace; it also affects how we live. Right behavior follows right belief, and right belief motivates right behavior.

THE HOW AND THE WHY OF GRACE IS JUST AS IMPORTANT AS THE WHAT

PETER CHALLENGES THE IDEA THAT grace should act in ignorance. Instead, grace should inspire holy living. Take David and Israel for example. They acted ignorant of God's commands about the ark of the covenant. Only after the death of Uzzah do they realize they weren't ignorant; they acted in ignorance. As followers of Christ, it's the same way.

Now as a parent, you have probably experienced moments where your child responds with "I didn't know..." Undoubtedly, there are moments where this is true. But there are also times when they are acting in ignorance but knew full well the expectation. This is what Peter is showing us. We are not ignorant of God's tremendous grace for us. As already stated, God's grace is the most radical, outrageous, revolutionary aspect of the gospel. It is this unique and startling message of God's grace that divides the real Christian faith from all other religions. And when we have been rescued by that grace, we should no longer live ignorantly about what God's grace is accomplishing in our lives.

If we are being honest, the spread of so many misapplied views has accelerated grace's idol form for most Christians. How many times have we heard sentences like "I'm not perfect. I'm just a simple sinner who received God's good grace." While that is certainly true, it's not entirely true. I am not a perfect Christian yet. Neither are you. None of us are. But I haven't just received God's grace as a sinner. I continue to receive God's grace as a saint. But the grace I receive as a saint moves me past where I was as a sinner. It takes away the "I'm just a sinner" excuse. Why? Because I now have knowledge of grace and I know it doesn't end there.

I would actually take this one step further. I would go so far as to say that it's rarely issues of skill, talent, or ability that take down so many Christians (especially Christian leaders). It's the places where we act ignorant. We know better, but we act anyway. Issues like compromise, burnout, pride, isolation, and hidden sin. We know that God's grace would never lead us there, but we ignorantly proceed.

Simply knowing God has given me grace is different than living it. If I grasp God's grace, I will gladly live differently. Instead of ignorance, grace acts as the "motor" that runs the engine of holiness. It causes us to run on all spiritual cylinders. This means that it's not just what I do but how and why I do it. Sometimes we think all God cares about is that we get things done, that perhaps he doesn't really care about how we do things. But grace tells us something different.

Notice in 1 Peter 1:15 Peter writes, "But as he who called you is holy, you also be holy in all your conduct." It says that God's grace moves God's holiness in us. Notice the phrase "in all your conduct." Holiness even spreads to the trivial details of our lives. By the way, isn't most of life made up of what seems like insignificant moments and small decisions? When it comes to living in grace, it often comes down to these small details.

For David and Israel, it was how they carried the ark. Instead, they grabbed the cart, rewrote the rules, and did it their own way. They made the ark an idol. This story would have been totally different if they did it right the first time. God's grace spreads to the how and why of our living. Am I obeying Christ out of obligation? Am I following without regard to motive? Why am I making this decision right now? Why am I reacting this way? Is this the best use of God's grace and reflection of God's holiness? We do well to ask these questions as we consider the how and why of grace.

When we think correctly about grace and live holy because of it, there will be many amazing gifts from God to experience and enjoy in our lives. The purpose of this book hasn't been to discourage you. Certainly, I pray it's been instructive and constructive, thought-provoking and challenging. But I also pray it's been inspiring and motivating. The truth is there is no greater journey than the life of grace. God's grace is remarkable...beyond description. But we have to have the eyes to see it correctly and a heart willing to follow it wherever it leads.

DON'T MISS THE SMALL GRACE-FILLED MOMENTS IN THE HERE AND NOW

SO MANY TIMES WE ARE constantly looking somewhere toward the future to hopefully see grace in a new light. Sometimes we can get so caught up in our daily existence that we fail to see its presence in our lives today. But it's at work all around us. In the small little moments with our families; in the tiny details of our workday; in the store when we're shopping; and when we are sitting in silence after a rough day. And every time we see it, it's pointing us back to the greatness of God.

Grace should enhance our awe of God. Maybe for you, it has become like the ark, a mere artifact of some moment in the past, or merely a promise of blessing in the future, instead of the God who is at work in you today. It should move you beyond the ho-hum, normal, and everyday life and point you to the One who is changing and completing you. It should cause you to see him more fully in the Scriptures; seek him more abundantly in your prayers; worship him more passionately in your music; see him more tenderly through your relationships; and share him more boldly to those who need him. Don't allow it to become more important than God. Don't allow grace to become an idol…a golden calf. Instead let grace bring you to a greater awareness of the magnificent Grace-Giver.

NOW WHAT?

Read: 2 Samuel 6; 1 Peter 1

Discuss:

1. Why were David and the people of Israel bringing the "ark of God" to Jerusalem? Why wasn't the ark in Jerusalem already?
2. Describe the importance of the "ark of the covenant" to the people of God? What did it represent? How did the ark remind Israel of God's grace?
3. Why did God act so strongly against Uzzah for doing what seemed to be a helpful deed? How does David's reaction and Israel's second attempt to bring the ark, demonstrate a change in their view about holiness?
4. How do we make grace common in our lives? How does connecting grace to God and his holiness keep it from becoming an idol? How has grace become common in your life?
5. Describe some of the grace-filled moments that are happening around you today:

Pray:

Pray that you would keep grace connected to the God who gives it.

Memorize/Meditate:

"Therefore, preparing your minds for action, and being sober-minded, set your hope fully on the grace that will be brought to you at the revelation of Jesus Christ." (1 Peter 1:13)